CW00664957

WOMEN IN MOVEMENTS
YESTERDAY, TODAY, TOMORROW

We are very greatful to *Le Débat* and *Passages* for allowing us to translate and publish the interview « Femmes en mouvements » and the articles by Antoinette Fouque.

ANTOINETTE FOUQUE

WOMEN IN MOVEMENTS
YESTERDAY, TODAY, TOMORROW

and other writings

des femmes

U.S.A.

1

WOMEN IN MOVEMENTS
yesterday, today, tomorrow*

translated by ANNE BERGER *and* ARTHUR DENNER

LE DÉBAT : Unlike many post-'68 political actors and some of your sisters of the Women's Movement, you have been silent. We know little about you. You are a figure of legend — a vivid reminder of the most outspoken wing of the M.L.F., (*Mouvement de Libération des Femmes*, Women's Liberation Movement),the *Psychanalyse et Politique* group, and yet a mystery...

ANTOINETTE FOUQUE : Even today, I suppose, anything that is connected with origins, which are always mythical, anything that remains of an initial orality, of the first words that are no longer heard, is seen as mysterious. Lacan used to say, « Parler, c'est déconner » (« To speak is to talk nonsense »)[1].
And as for writing... !
As you know, what came to be called the Women's Liberation Movement, the M.L.F., was created on the

---

*An interview by MARCEL GAUCHET and PIERRE NORA, in *Le débat* n° 59, Gallimard, Mars-Avril, 1990.

heels of '68. With the events of '68 themselves, even. May '68 was first and foremost an effervescence, an oral explosion, a cry ; for me — and not only for me — it was a birth ; perhaps that's why it is still burdened with so many mysteries. The Women's Movement may well have been started by intellectuals — Monique Wittig, Josiane Chanel and myself — but the cry came first, and with the cry the body ; a body so harshly put down by the society of the 1960s, so violently repressed by the masters of contemporary thought, by those who at the time were modern.

Monique was already a recognized writer. As for me, I was working with literary journals, *Cahiers du Sud, Le Mercure de France, La Quinzaine littéraire.* I was reading manuscripts for a publisher. But the Movement did not begin with the written word, it began with what used to be called « la prise de parole », taking the floor and speaking out, with protests and slogans of revolt, words from the body. I used to say at the time that the revolution that the Women's movement was going to bring about would consist in lifting the censorship of the body — just as in psychoanalytic practice and theory Freud had lifted the censorship of the unconscious — and, naturally, would thereby enrich the text, just as Freud had wanted to enrich the conscious mind.

But when you talk about a mysterious, legendary figure, you are, I think, going beyond me and raising the question of origin. It is an immense question that we could discuss for hours and which would touch not only on our contemporaries' relationships to that question but also on the relationship that I myself, who was present at the origin of the M.L.F. (a moment that certain women historians today call its prehistory), have with my own origins, on real, as well as fantastic and symbolic levels. I used to go so far as to say that women's civilizing development would take us from prehistory to posthistory. The relationship that our contemporaries still maintain with the question of origin is one of fear or rejection, which tends to be confused with the fear of women, or of a woman : some analysts have used the term *fantasmère* (phantasmother) to speak of that archaic figure. That was its heyday, for at the time the Women's movement excluded men, to re-mark our exclusion from most institutions and achieve status through opposition. It was virtually impossible to do otherwise. To refer to an earlier time in history, perhaps the erudite might, in this particular context remember more or less vaguely that other A. Fouque — Adelaïde and not Antoinette, but nonetheless an Aixoise, a new Eve, bearer of sin and hated by her creator — who is at the origin of Zola's monumental work, *Les Rougon-Macquart...*

I have to say that I was ill-served by the way in which the Movement tended to close itself up — or off — as I have explained, and also by my own shut-in nature which had to do, since my adolescence, with my motor difficulties and with the pain and effort it cost me to get around, to get where sometimes I had to be : demonstrations, dinners, social gatherings, all of that was prohibited because I had to save my strength for my work.

And then what can only be called the unconscious root of misogyny, the foreclosure of origin, or rather , as I have always stressed, the foreclosure of the body of the mother as the site of the origin of life, was redoubled by my own relationship to my origins : there were

9

my psychic relationship to my sexual origins, homo-sexed vis-à-vis the woman who was my mother and heterosexed vis-à-vis the man who was my father, and my political relationship to my historical, social and cultural origins. A complex, even composite, relationship to an origin — I have written « an origins », just as I have written « a women » — to a heterogeneous origin.

This relationship of rupture or connection with an origin, including one's own origin, it would seem to me, orients each individual's destiny. This, for me, is at the crux of it all, it is the very goal of the work of the body and carnal thought. And it seems to me that as long as the investigation of this relationship — a necessarily ambiguous investigation — does not take place, all we have is a monosexual and therefore lobotomized humanism.

I myself am trying to set origins in motion through a continual labor of « regression-reintegration » instead of repression or even foreclosure. It is like labor in pregnancy, a kind of intimate dynamic, an elementary movement.

As for « mysterious », from the Eleusinian mysteries to Freud and his « black continent », « mysterious » is the term that man comes up with wherever there is woman ; *mutatis mutandi*, it could even be the certificate of authenticity that attests to the insistence or even existence of woman. One day, the sciences of woman, gyneco-nomy in particular, will perhaps take up this mystery, will think it through, reduce it and explain it, bring it as much as possible to consciousness, and will understand it and interpret it. What does the dream of the romantic have in common with the dream in the Freudian interpretation ? More or less what the Eleusinian mysteries have in common with a science of women.

LE DÉBAT : What were you doing on the eve of '68?

ANTOINETTE FOUQUE : I was apparently an ordinary French teacher on long-term disability leave and, in fact, a rebel. I was beginning my third year of doctoral studies, working with Roland Barthes on my thesis, which I never finished, on the notion of a literary avant-garde. I had arrived in 1960 from Aix-en-Provence, was married to an intellectual the same age as I. My daughter was four. He and I were working for François Wahl at *Le Seuil*[2]. My work, preparing reader's reports, was an education for me in difficult disciplines — linguistics, psychoanalysis, antipsychiatry —, and I kept abreast of the most recent contemporary texts : Sanguinetti, Balestrini, Porta, which I even translated. My future seemed clear ; everything seemed to point me toward publishing, criticism, writing.

But in fact, I was very rebellious. A woman's economic independence, professional equality, intellectual competence were not really valued. The milieu in which I found myself was very conservative in the way it operated, its modernist theorizings were in fact repressive and intimidating, and so it was extremely misogynistic. I was constantly made aware of the false promise of equality, symmetry and reciprocity that a university education had for so long held out. To have had a baby was almost shameful. Beyond that spurious equality, I felt other needs arising. I wanted to affirm in a positive way that I was a woman, since society, I might even say civilization, was penalizing me for being one.

LE DÉBAT : And it was in that context that you met Lacan ?

ANTOINETTE FOUQUE : Yes. Through François Wahl, I had participated in the publication of the *Écrits :* it was an interminable labor, over two years. I was also attending his seminar, along with Roland Barthes's.

LE DÉBAT : What about analysis ?

ANTOINETTE FOUQUE : I got in touch with Lacan in October 1968, at the time of our first meetings. My analysis began in January 1969 and continued until 1974.

LE DÉBAT : Did you feel before '68 that you were a feminist ?

ANTOINETTE FOUQUE : It never occurred to me to use that word. I felt like a woman who badly needed to be free, who was suffering, but every « ism » seemed like a trap to me.
Ever since I was a small child, I questioned the lot of women. I was born of the desire of a working-class father, in 1936, which began as the year of victory for him and ended with bitter defeats. I was conceived on the 1st of January and born on the 1st of October, on the day Franco came to power in Spain. I come from a big family — part Corsican and part Calabrian. We were something of a tribe. There was my father and my mother, my father's brother and my mother's sister — godfather and godmother — and the four children. My mother was one of a kind, but I grew up surrounded by the strength of maternal women. From very early on, I was aware of their endurance,

their courage and their determination to integrate themselves — and with them their children — without disowning themselves.

My mother didn't know how to read or write and that was her constant complaint — she spoke of it as though it were her greatest misfortune. My father could read a newspaper. They were very civilized people, of the old school ; I could almost call them « cultivated », because of their Mediterranean roots. That is one of the most paradoxical aspects of my highly problematic relationship with writing. (One of the reasons why I went to see Lacan was that he was the author of the *Ecrits*, as Montaigne was the author of *Essais*, but without ever having wanted to write a book.)

My mother became French through marriage and was very proud of that. She considered it a sign of progress to have traded the Italian name of her father for her husband's Corsican name. Yet she never forgot her matrilineal genealogy. Neither have I. Just as my mother named me after her mother, I named my daughter after mine. Over four generations, we seem to have been careful to establish a transmission, to inscribe another lineage. This was well before the M.L.F., and I used to say that I was a woman who was trying to find herself between mother and daughter, between woman and woman.

My mother is the most intelligent woman I have known, as well as the most independent. She had a kind of genius for freedom, for freedom without violence. Her mind was always at work. From a very young age, I could see, in spite of a total absence of the trappings of femininity in her — she didn't wear make up, she wasn't flirtatious, and she didn't care at all to be elegant or stylish — that my mother was a woman. My father adored her, silently. He would whistle the tunes of love songs to her ; she knew the words. They met when she was sixteen and he eighteen and they always had, right until the end, a sort of youthful passion, even though he had the temperament of the virile patriarch. During the war, my father had been locally banned because while he was on strike, Pétain's police had found him with his Communist Party card on him. Just as my mother, during the first World War, had, as the eldest child, stood fast with her brothers and sisters, now under the occupation, she took the whole tribe under her wing. In the most serious, the most dramatic situations, she managed to find escape routes and safe havens. She led us away from death. She was never inert but always active. She could sense when there was danger ahead, would assess it ; when there was a decision to be made she was decisive she would make her move, taking us in tow. She was in charge twenty-four hours a day, always alert but not authoritarian in the least — angry sometimes but most often serious yet cheerful. For example, when we were bombed out or had been evacuated when Marseille's Vieux-Port district was destroyed, she proved to be a real strategist, as subtle and crafty as Ulysses.

LE DÉBAT : When '68 happened, were you aware of what was going on in American feminism ?

ANTOINETTE FOUQUE : Not at all. I had opened *The Second Sex* in the sixties only to read : « Women's struggles are behind us ». I had never been politically active. I knew that I was born a leftist and would die a leftist, that I hated war and colonialism. Until I reached adulthood, I was part of what was still called the working class, but I never felt drawn to Sartrean *engagement*, to the « guilty conscience » of the intellectual.

I was concerned about social and political struggles, but at a distance. I observed them as though through a pane of glass. I could never manage to feel implicated in them and felt a kind of disgust for the young women of my generation who got involved in the struggles of their lovers, their brother *normaliens*[3], which was how I felt about my sister who, when she got engaged, tried to convince herself that she was a soccer fan.

I didn't know what feminism was and now I can say that I regret that. It was a sign of my ignorance of the struggles of women in history. But I should emphasize that my distrust of ideologies — which, at the time, I considered to be illusions as dangerous as religion — was such that I never defined myself as a feminist. Later, I fought against the Women's Movement becoming the « Feminist Movement ». It seemed to me, perhaps wrongly, that with the word *woman* we might be able to reach if not all women, at least the greatest number possible.

LE DÉBAT : But wasn't the name *Psychanalyse et Politique* rather elitist ?

ANTOINETTE FOUQUE : I didn't choose that name ; one usually doesn't get to choose the name one is given at birth. But *Psychanalyse et Politique* was what used to be called a consciousness-raising group ; not that we were unaware of the unconscious, at the level of what Freud called the psychopathology of everyday life, humor, or parapraxis. And at that time, you'll recall, everyone was talking about desire, anti-psychiatry, anti-Œdipus ; and at Vincennes[4], psychoanalysis was taught outdoors. Our claim to express ourselves to each other felt more like luxury rather than elitism.

One of the things I wanted, at that time, was to bring to as many people as possible what was then the cutting edge of contemporary thought, in other words, to transcend the stereotypes of petit-bourgeois culture.

I wanted to share with any woman who came to the Movement, just as I had done with the women in my family, with my mother in particular. I wanted to find a common language without bowing down to class stereotypes or academic ideals. But the road to hell is paved with good intentions, and just the opposite happened : I was accused of being a theoretical terrorist, a terrorist of theory ; only my accusers weren't workers but sociologists, academics who were very hostile to psychoanalysis.

Le Débat : What were you doing during the days of '68 ?

Antoinette Fouque : Monique Wittig and I were at the Sorbonne. We formed a Cultural Action Committee that drew filmmakers, actors, writers, intellectuals : Bulle Ogier, Michèle Moretti, André Téchiné, Danièle Delorme, Marguerite Duras — these are just a few of the names that come to mind.

Le Débat : You were thirty-two years old then. You found yourselves in the position of elder sisters to the generation of '68, properly speaking. With seniority, doesn't there naturally come the power to influence...

ANTOINETTE FOUQUE : You mean in the M.L.F. ? Age distinctions were even less important there than at the Sorbonne in May. We were all young and beautiful. For most of us, it was our first involvement in politics. We felt as though we had grown fifteen years younger. We all felt in '68 as though we had come down with a healthy case of adolescence. Later, we fought systematically against age distinctions. At our meetings, high school girls rubbed shoulders joyously with Christiane Rochefort, as women workers did with women engineers, and daughters with mothers.

LE DÉBAT : Did you feel at ease right away in a political environment ?

ANTOINETTE FOUQUE : The truth is that if Monique hadn't dragged me by the scruff of the neck, I would never have gone to the Sorbonne. I was very intimidated. I had never spoken in public, except in class. That probably explains, in my own case and for many others, a tone and manner that was simultaneously vibrant and excessive — it was an clumsy revolt, it had been held in check too long.

LE DÉBAT : And from there to the Women's Movement as such ?

ANTOINETTE FOUQUE : Monique and I quickly learned from our experience at the Sorbonne that if we did not ask our own questions, on our own terms, we would be dominated or excluded. For the first time in my life, it was necessary and urgent for me to anchor myself in a decisive historical moment in which my personal history started to come into play. It was a need to intervene, to give something to others and also to give something to myself, to act out of gratitude as well as out of egotism. That's what made it different from a leftist type of involvement. During the summer of '68, over the holidays, we decided to begin meeting in October. We then set about to read and critique, with whatever means we had at our disposal, the works of Marx, Engels, Lenin, but we found their doctrines entirely unsuitable. We were set on freeing ourselves from the constraints of our domestic, professional and emotional lives. We wanted to expand the field of our subjectivity. We wanted to embark on the discovery of women through the discovery of each woman, beginning with ourselves. We got on board the Maoist-Leninist Marxist cause, but we were rowing against the current.

LE DÉBAT : When did you make the further leap represented by the choice of the *Psychoanalysis and Politics* orientation ?

ANTOINETTE FOUQUE : Almost immediately, since we were reading Freud, too. But I must admit that, though not uncritical, I let myself be dazzled by the undertaking. The masculine ideology that weighed upon the psychoanalytic revolution wasn't enough to make me reject such a tool of knowledge, especially if that meant erecting a counter-ideology, an ideology of feminism. I couldn't see myself, in this high-seas adventure, trading Freud's submarine for the scooter of some feminist, even a famous one. Especially since both of them, it seemed to me, were headed in the same direction — straight for the Phallus — but with the feminists, you weren't allowed to be aware of it or to point out the shoals. It seemed to me that if we didn't take the unconscious into account, we would soon be drifting right into delirium. *Psych et Po* reflected my desire to understand the unconscious aspects of the political engagements of the time, as well as to bring out into the open the power of psychoanalysis, not only in institutions and schools but also in the discovery of the unconscious and its theorization. I thought it vital that politics know and question the unconscious, and vice versa. Simply put, there was politics in the unconscious and the unconscious in politics. Since then, I have often thought of it as a sort of parental couple that brought me into the world of time and place : psychoanalysis is my mother with her inquisitive intimacy and watchful anguish, and politics is my father with his proletarian revolt, his commitment to resistance. A couple continually coupling and uncoupling so that both might affirm the uniqueness of their individual fields and the identity of their separate bodies, so that he might give to her, the woman, a political existence, so that she might make him, the man, conscious of his dreams.

LE DÉBAT : There was a period of gestation before the movement went public...

ANTOINETTE FOUQUE : Yes. For two years, we worked intensively among ourselves : we met, wrote tracts, put out information... Our first public appearance — there were thirty of us — took place on March 30, 1970 at Vincennes. For me, that was the public debut. Because there was another as well, which took place at the Arc de Triomphe, to commemorate « the unknown soldier's unknown wife ». I wasn't there, and that was no accident. This was a media event with three celebrities and almost no one else. Those two events, Vincennes and the Arc de Triomphe, point up the divergent paths that lay before the Movement.

Following our going public, I was offered a lectureship at Vincennes, which I accepted. With the start of the school year in 1970, we began meeting in this broader setting. The Movement began to snowball. Other small groups joined ours.

LE DÉBAT : Tell us about your meeting with Simone de Beauvoir.

ANTOINETTE FOUQUE : For a long time, she was suspicious of the Movement, even hostile. The impetus for the meeting came from the feminists but it was she who convened those who were, in her words, its « leaders ». I really had to be coaxed because I couldn't understand this way of going about things. She asked us to explain to her our conception of a women's movement.

Sartre, at the time, was taking up leftist causes. Perhaps there was a desire for symmetry. Perhaps he had explained to her the stakes and the importance of an uprising like this, just as he had incited her to write *The Second Sex* after his *Anti-Semite and Jew*. Ingenuously, we presented our hopes and our dreams. I spoke of my daughter, I spoke of Lacan, of Barthes, and especially of Derrida. I admired his ideas and most of the time the texts of those about whom he wrote, from Leroi-Gourhan to Blanchot. I did not go over very well, to say the least. Even though I felt a kind of deference toward the intellectual persona of Simone de Beauvoir, for her stubborn desire to be at

Sartre's side, the couple's life that she was living struck me as hardly exemplary or enviable. I had admired *The Mandarins* ; I found it difficult to take that she could be turned into the laughing stock of a clan of misogynist intellectuals. But at the time, I couldn't understand why this stubborn moralist, this lofty conscience, had not joined the Resistance during the war ; why, during the occupation, between her bicycle trips and her climbing excursions around Marseilles, she spent her time getting her manuscripts published at Gallimard, which at the time was controlled by the Nazis. Ultimately, nothing was said, but my plea that our Movement take into account psychoanalysis as the only rigorous discourse on sexuality clearly placed me in the wrong camp. Not long afterwards, at our general meeting, the feminists were shouting for heads — mine on the end of a pike, and Simone de Beauvoir's to lead *Les femmes s'entêtent* [« The Headstrong Women »][5].

Many of us experienced it as a hostile takeover bid. It was like an occupation, or if you wish, a colonization, but we managed to resist « Revolutionary Feminist Movement » by insisting on « women » and « liberation ». Actually, I don't like talking about Simone de Beauvoir. Just as it is often said that the greatness of an enemy in fair combat does us honor, I have often said to myself that the unfairness of her attacks has made me feel ashamed.

LE DÉBAT : What exactly lay behind the rift over the word « feminist » ?

ANTOINETTE FOUQUE : It has been said in recent years that the Movement had two orientations, one towards equality, the other towards identity. I want to make it clear, right from the start, that identity in this context must be understood as the uniqueness of the other and not as sameness.

For many, the best way of fighting oppression and the discrimination that comes from sexual difference and dissymmetry was to abolish difference, to deny dissymmetry. To my mind, that was like throwing out the baby with the bath water. The rallying cry « One out of every two men is a woman » then became « A woman is a man like any other ». It seemed that the only alternative to exclusion was assimilation. This return to an absolute universalism, this militancy for indifference, seemed to me preanalytic and archaic, given how far contemporary thinking had come. The notion of equality is still quite sketchy. It has to be put to work, set in motion. Those who favored integration exclusively now know its limits. I could say, for example, that equality is the basis for difference, or rather its impetus : it is the motor of future differences. Difference keeps it in check. It's something like the relationship between consciousness and the unconscious. Consciousness is the tip of the iceberg, the part we can see, just as equality is the visible part of differences. Consciousness without the unconscious is only an illusion of intelligence, and equality without difference is a ruinous theoretical delusion.

But I avoided the word « identity » which lent itself to misinterpretation at a time when the subject was on trial ; it might have been confused with the identical, with sameness, whereas the thing was to get away from that, to find a decentered position, each one of us, woman and man, according to her or his own uniqueness. Individualistic feminism seemed to me to be saying : « The same model for everyone, and everyone for herself ». As for us, ours was the utopia of « each according to her own uniqueness, together ».

LE DÉBAT : How do you remember those divisive and controversial years ?

ANTOINETTE FOUQUE : Truly frightful. And quite cruel... Most of the time, my adversaries wouldn't engage with me in discussion — their pretext was that every discussion ended with me being right. I never responded to those attacks by going outside the M.L.F., except later, when we were accused — our publishing house was the pretext — of being a sect of thieves and criminals. Even though I refused to make a personal issue out of it and left it up to the court, through the intermediary of George Kiejman. It was very destructive, but no more so than any political confrontation can be. I suffered as much as I would have had I been living under a bombardment, I lost the last of my motor capabilities, but I learned a lot.

The psychoanalytic work helped me not to drown in hate or in terror ; it helped me to symbolize, to swim, to live. The name « feminist », some women have said, gave them a sense of unity, a dynamic feeling of belonging, a strong ego, and our approach to the issues was like a wet blanket on all that. Our questions destabilized, and that is why the disputes were so bitter. But why should women do away with aggressivity, violence, and hatred, and settle a priori into the most disturbing kind of monochromatic Stalinist pacifism ?

LE DÉBAT : All of this became connected with your analysis with Lacan.

ANTOINETTE FOUQUE : As I have said, my analysis helped me to « roam » instead of foundering in leftist-feminist impasses. It freed me from my adherence to all kinds of illusions which were as perverse for me as they were innocent for others. My analysis kept me decentered, which naturally was painful. It kept me withdrawn for the most part, and silent, kept me in a dissymmetry that was fruitful for me but disturbing for everyone who felt that it didn't go with, that it somehow clashed with *Psych et Po*. Were they faced with a new sect. Well, that's because they represented the reigning dogma...

LE DÉBAT : And yet the *École freudienne* itself started to function like a sect of particularly blind followers...[6]

ANTOINETTE FOUQUE : In my analysis with Lacan, I was always very free with my criticisms. I believe he appreciated it, that it helped advance his work, and that, without the M.L.F., he wouldn't have written *Encore*. I used to go to all his seminars. I also attended his closed clinical seminars at Sainte-Anne [psychiatric hospital] where he presented his patients. He wanted to enroll me himself in that seminar, but I never wanted to belong to the *École freudienne* any more than I wanted to belong to a political party. I had enough to do coping with my inhibitions, my symptoms, my anxieties, without having to deal with institutional constraints, without having to join a group of major intimidators.

We had so much to do to establish our own laws

within the law, to get away from the outlaw status to which women are confined, to escape our foreclosure, even more than our exclusion, and we felt so small, so inexperienced, so clumsy... It seemed so easy to drive us to the point where we would start to kill each other. We would have prefered that it remain a fight, if not a debate, of ideas. But apart from Simone de Beauvoir, who changed from the figure of ridicule that she had been in the sixties into an intellectual master, unbeatable, as some of her journalist groupies have written, there were many clans out there to whose advantage it was that this turn into a fight for pure prestige, a battle to the death for a power that we didn't have then any more than we will have it tomorrow or the day after... And yet, at the same time, it was like a Ferris wheel, a moment of destabilizing but also joyous giddiness, a chaotic and productive education, an exhausting and exalting apprenticeship to life and history.

LE DÉBAT : We won't dwell on the most familiar aspects of the Movement : the series of publications beginning with *Le Torchon brûle* [« The dishcloth burns »] in 1970, and especially of course, the struggle for abortion rights. But just a word or two on that subject. Didn't a media strategy, the kind that you don't like, ultimately pay off in the famous « Manifeste des 343 »[7] ?

ANTOINETTE FOUQUE : I recognize that, and I acknowledged it right away at the time. I wouldn't have approached things that way at the time. It was the feminists who had the idea of including celebrities in the manifesto, following the leftist model. That was

ANTOINETTE FOUQUE

very positive, but it hasn't made me any less distrust-
ful of the media, who have made me pay. My idea was
just a little idealistic. It was not a desire to hide but
rather a need not to go on display. My dream was that
thought and action could go forward hand in hand, at
a slow and confident pace, that we were going to nar-
row the gap between those who slaved away in obs-
curity and the stars who took the spotlight and put
on the show. I'm always delighted when a famous
personality joins in a struggle, providing she brings to
it more than she takes away ; what worries me is the
way famous names can capitalize on a cause to which
they are not committed and still profit from it. It was
that kind of narcissistic speculation that we were
faced with ; first we had bank credit cards, and now
we have media credit cards, via various associations
and groupings. Watch out for inflation, roll-overs, and
the market crash of narcissism ! It's not that I refused
to acknowledge the importance and the validity of
the media, but at the time, they wanted to dictate to
us, to foist new stereotypes on us, and I saw no
shame in not rushing off after them. I not only signed
the manifesto, but I also actively fought for legal and
free abortion.

Le Débat : And it was after that victory, the passage
of the legalized abortion law, that you wanted to further the Movement by creating the publishing house
des femmes ?

Antoinette Fouque : It was a dream I had had since
the Movement began. The negative battles that had to
be fought, the struggles against, the fight to defeat
oppression, gave me only very limited and ambivalent

26

satisfaction. I signed the abortion manifesto out of solidarity and conviction ; the Veil law was vital for all of us[8], but I could never have an abortion. From the beginning, I wanted to build, to bring into being, to lay out positive paths. I wanted to emphasize women's creative power, to show that women enrich civilization, and that they are not merely the keepers of hearth and home, shut up in a community of the oppressed. I wanted to open the Movement up to the public : to publish. My dream was not only a publishing house but also a bookstore, apublic place open to men as well as women. I knew that even the most scrupulous publishers choose manuscripts according to criteria that penalized women. The first text that we published had been rejected by other publishers. As you know, the experience brought us more envy than either thanks from women or admiration from men. I believe that during those dark years only François Maspero suffered as much as we did. But to be circumspect about it, I think that things could not have gone otherwise.

LE DÉBAT : How would you assess this entreprise ? At the time, there was much talk about promoting an *écriture feminine*. What are your thoughts on the project and its outcome today.

ANTOINETTE FOUQUE : To put the best face on things, I suppose that the wise thing to do with the entreprise would be to fold... The last ten years have been a hard time for publishers. As for *écriture feminine*, once again, we weren't the ones to come up with the expression. I think that it's a French translation of the expression « female writing ». But in French, *la femelle*, hasn't been a human category for several centuries now ; in other words, the woman, in French, has lost the integrity of her sex. After having been completely sequestered in her uterus for thousands of years, it now turns out that she doesn't have one, that she is merely gender, the other metaphor for phallic monism. The human female is foreclosed from our language, a phallic language if ever there was. Thus the feminine is a gender that many men — from the transvestite to the poet, that imaginary transsexual — feel they can assume. We can read femininity in Rilke's writing, or in Rimbaud's. It's not simple... A human being is born with a sex, a girl or a boy, but also as a speaking being. Our experiences, our actions are constantly informed by this physiological determinism. For the man as well as for the woman, physiology is destiny. But at every moment, what we say or what we write either conforms to or dissents from the constraints that the body imposes on language and on the fantasies that language produces in its speakers.

One is born a girl or a boy, and then becomes a woman or a man, masculine or feminine ; to write will therefore never be a gender-neutral act. Anatomical destiny is always being marked, marked out or re-marked. Gender differences come along and validate or invalidate sexual differences. How can the writing or the experience of a sexually differentiated subject be neutral ? We did not want to put the cart before the horse. We accepted the challenge, took the risk of proposing that texts written by women might put the language to work in ways that perhaps could bring out — indeed, why not ? — a sexual difference. We never set out to declare as a foregone conclusion that there was such a thing as women's writing. When Kundera, in *The Art of the Novel*, speculates as to how he might use the word « contraband » to smuggle into Czech the French word for having an erection, *bander*, what is he talking about, what is he doing ? Lacan, too, said that language has only that on its mind. What is « that » ? Having a hard on ? And in the meantime, how do women find their pleasure ? For millenia, men have been working on symbolizing and inscribing their phallic libidos. I remember a wonderful text by Pierre Guyotat, « *L'autre main branle* » [« The other hand jerks off »]. They could certainly wait a few decades, give us a few centuries, to find an equivalent work by women... But then again, this *écriture féminine* that everyone bandies about has been used as an ultimate weapon, a cream pie to be thrown in the face of top flight writers who didn't wait either for the M.L.F. or *des femmes* to come into being before setting forth their poetics. I'm thinking specifically of Hélène Cixous : *Inside*, which won her the Prix Médicis in 1969, carried within it the seed of everything she would write later.

LE DÉBAT : What about the Women's Movement today ? It seems to have been swept along with the general ebbing of the spirit of '68.

ANTOINETTE FOUQUE : The Movement was a creature of '68 which took its stance against the tide of extreme leftism and now is going to go far beyond it, just as it is now surmounting the symbolic Restoration that has come with the eighties. You don't need me to tell you that upheavals of such scope do not play themselves out in ten or twenty years. It is not about changes, in the sense of a changeover ; it is about the species' crisis of growth. We are at the heart of civilization's famous discontent, the passage from one stage to another, in which women find themselves involved against their will, taken hostage, and made to serve as the symptom of the Other's madness. This is what is happening to Salman Rushdie. You go as far as you can at any given moment, given the array of forces and what history can handle. It may later seem like a ebbing but this is deceptive. New paths are opening up, there is groundwater yet from which new inspiration can be drawn. There will be new ways of transcribing what seems illegible to us today. Through progredient regressions, perhaps sometimes, women are still advancing. After ten or fifteen years of State feminism (Françoise Giroud was named Secretary of State for the Condition of Women in 1974), the founding militants could very well demobilize ; it was even vital that they did so, so that new voices could be heard and new steps could be taken. Most have done so.

The many levels of resistance — subjective and objective, psychic, emotional, political and narcissistic — to this movement of civilization are now obvious. Resistance, in politics as in analysis, functions in complex and polyvalent ways, and is part of a healthy maturation process.

The paths to symbolization — a term I prefer to « sublimation » — are complex. Creation and invention are necessarily paradoxical. Freud, who for half a century theorized the talking cure, spent the last several years of his life with a cancer of the jaw which prevented him from speaking. His daughter

Anna, his Antigone, delivered his lectures for him. You asked that I give you a personal example. I could say that my movement, which I have never confused with my mobility, is certainly not unrelated to my paralysis. I am afflicted with one of those forgotten illnesses, for which still today there is no cure. I've probably had it, latently, since birth or before, and it manifested itself after a vaccination that I had when I had finished school. The neurologists warned me that one day very soon I'd be confined to a wheelchair. I've managed to put off that day for more than thirty years, with a lot of effort to adapt to a « normal » life. Analysis has, of course, helped me in this. But perhaps at times it has over-immobilized me. And the movement which has taken so much of my strength has also given me so much. And finally, perhaps I can say that, just as thirst teaches us water, immobility has taught me movement.

The destructive forces came from without. Dialogue among ourselves may have been difficult, but it was made destructive by people who were interested in taking the conflict outside. Everyone knows that fraternity can breed fratricide. But no one — except the right wing — thinks of using the internal fights among the various tendencies of the Socialist Party to destroy this one or that one. But that didn't go for us. Our differences, which after all were quite normal, were used to discredit us. It seemed that everything we did or said had to be held against us. The misogynists were right to defend themselves, the stakes are very real. We simply didn't think there would be so many of them, that they would find so many women to be their accomplices. Every little group, every party, every clique, tried to manipulate and control us, tried to take advantage of us. Each organization yielded up its own feminism. Perhaps it was a sign that that ideology was politically and symbolically dependent on the phallic structure. On the horizon was the mirage of equality that, since 1789, offered the illusion of a Promised Land attainable through a class struggle that no one believed in anymore.

LE DÉBAT : One could in good faith, according to a certain logic, consider that universality is more liberating than an identity that imprisons women in their biological determinacy.

ANTOINETTE FOUQUE : Why should biological determinacies continue to be a prison for women ? Shouldn't it be just the opposite, from the moment that one has control over one's fertility ? After all, if anatomy is destiny, that also holds true for men. The reality principle cannot ignore those determinacies and a just society would not exploit them. Equality and difference must go hand in hand ; one cannot be sacrified for the other. Sacrificing equality for difference takes us back to the reactionary positions of traditional societies, and sacrificing sexual difference — and along with it, the richness of life that it brings — for equality sterilizes women and impoverishes humanity as a whole. It makes it impossible to reach the stage of symbolic genitality. This should be understood as a metaphor and not as some kind of psychobiological reductionism. Genial and geni(t)al, it's the same word, isn't it ? When we recognize the genius of scientists or artists, we admire their ability to produce some living signifier, to bring into the world a form, an element, a unique flesh that didn't exist before they created it. These « geniuses » have always used procreative metaphors in talking about their work. It seems to me that the notion of equality has never to this day been adequately articulated. Once, I would have called it an idealistic concept. We never found the model to be of much relevance when we fought with women in Latin America or in the Maghreb, except on the level of labor issues ; even so, women who in their professional lives enjoy the benefits of equal rights suffer a de facto penalization because of the dissymmetry inherent in procreation, a dissymmetry that at first no one wanted to take into account . One day, procreation will be seen as a creation of « speaking-living » matter, will be recognized as an important contribution of riches that is brought by women to the human community, a contribution that they bring for themselves, not only as a physiological psychosexual maturity but as a possibility of a free fulfillment of desire. That's reality for the majority of women, and if some of us, without having to give anything up, also write books or become Prime Minister, so much the better.

LE DÉBAT : Couldn't it simply have been the considerable success of the Women's Movement in social areas that led to the demoblization of its activists ?

ANTOINETTE FOUQUE : You're probably right. Even if today it has lost some of its momentum, it's a movement that history will say was a success. And yet the official documents (the UNESCO report), the surveys, the analyses in the media, everything indicates setbacks, exclusion, threats and the repression of women. More than acts of resistance, what we see just about everywhere are counter-movements. Basic misogynistic oppression has been succeeded by an anti-emancipatory repression. The normative prohibitions on which our societies are founded are turning perversely against women's new freedoms. I'm thinking not only of what is a totally political alliance of the three monotheisms, but also of the return of Œdipus, the demanding, abusive parricide son, served up to us by the media in some new guise every day : so-and-so, thirty-eight years old, rapes his sixty-eight year old mother ; someone else, thirty-six years old brings a suit against his mother for having abandoned him ; another man, younger, kills his girlfriend because she was more successful than he ; and so on and so forth. Criminality has a sex. Men who want to remain in their protracted state of infantile omnipotence are afraid of women. Women are afraid because they're in mortal danger. From Althusser[9] to Paulin, who killed old women, to Karlin's hero[10], crimes are constantly being justified or excused through powerful identification fantasies. Whether they're delusional or passionate, criminals or artists, the sons « identify » the sons with utter brutality and complete impunity.

It will no doubt be more difficult for women to free themselves from the son than from the father, who to my mind, does not exist as such ; it's hard to cast off the role of Jocasta, to escape the passion according to St. Œdipus. The temptation to redeem the murderer will be great — that's a very feminine way of escaping castration. Have a child and keep him for herself, raving mad or autistic, as a phallus with whom to shut herself up outside herself and in an exile of the self, rather than producing a child and letting him set off on his own destiny as a man.

LE DÉBAT : Let's return to '68. In retrospect, how do you understand the movement of '68 and where do you situate the Women's Movement within it ?

ANTOINETTE FOUQUE : I experienced '68 as a real revolution and as time goes by, I'm more and more convinced of this : it was the great leap out of the capitalist era, which has little left for it today other than to complete itself or, better yet, to finish itself off worldwide. '68 was the end of the era of economics as the ultimate determinant, both for liberalism and for Marxism. And along with that end, *exit* de Gaulle, the father and president-founder of that most monarchical republic, who, almost two hundred years after the regicide, they suddenly realized was only a son. There is no father. May '68 was the first time the sons came together as such ; after liberty and equality, enter the *era of fraternity*. The demands of phallo-narcissism were written everywhere on all the walls. Remember those two posters — « Power comes at the end of a gun » one of them went ; the other said « Power comes at the end of the phallus » — and those graffiti of erect penises that joyously covered the walls of the Sorbonne, the Latin Quarter and then Vincennes. All of them self-portraits of the extreme-leftist as young Narcissus or old Priapus. I firmly believe that the priapism of leftism is something that's been definitely overlooked.

Linked to the narcissistic valorization of the penis, the so-called phallic phase establishes a logic according to which, for the boy, only those like himself who possess the same prestigious organ are worthy of respect : the double, the reflection, the twin, the brother, or these days, the buddy. A chain of identifications among all those that glitter : the golden boys get the gold and the phallus. You can't get the former without the latter any more, but it's the latter that manufactures and attracts the former. The phallus presides over gold. That is what is new.

What is at stake in what Freud called the « primacy of the phallus » is something that for both sexes is essentially narcissistic in nature. This logic can therefore be termed phallo-narcissistic. The omnipotence and omnipresence of the phallus can also be represented by the fetish, which, as Freud says, is erected as a « memorial » before the horror of the supposedly female or maternal castration, which is pure denial, upheld today by universal commodification, the generalized exhibition of « nomadic objects », the ownership of gadgets, of prostheses ; pure denial because how can this woman-mother have lost a penis that she never had except in his, the son-and-man's, perverse imagination.

The phallus is the emblem, the image, the master signifier, the general equivalent of narcissistic wholeness. A woman, when she finds herself deprived of a « libido of one's own », is subjected to its imperialism, to its mode of economic development. If she is not satisfied with being an Echo, then she has no other choice for self-expression other than to take that path, but at the expense of her psychic and physiological integrity ; she commits her body to it, or rather, she is given notice that she must surrender her body as a hostage and succumb to a pathology in which she will be seen by herself and by others as the phallus — body and soul, bodies like those very erect, obelisk-like bodies, that one still sees today in many movie actresses and models, souls like those God-

Paternal souls that many women writers or government ministers seem to have. And that's how women, with or without the chador, get caught in the trap of a phallic narcissism that has little to do with them and become its most perfect symptom.

Christianity is a filiarchy, a religion of the son, a filial monotheism, one might say. Socialism is perhaps its secular version. As you can imagine, in such a climate women have not had an easily defined place, given that nothing excludes girls more than brotherhoods do. Girls can always, by identifying with the sons, dress themselves up as "she-sons" (*"filse"*, the French word for "son" written in the feminine gender), but there again, symmetry is an illusion and a trap. If you've ever experienced the atmosphere of condescension towards women in groups of the extreme left, you understand this. Their women militants came to the M.L.F. to complain about this, just so that they could escape dangerous identifications. Women in France who have sided with violent groups or supported terrorism are rare indeed. The feminists from *Action Directe*[11] came by once or twice to wreck the *des Femmes* bookstore, but the analysis of ambient violence, an analysis to which the Movement as a whole and not only « *Psych et Po* » was committed, served as a powerful brake on the all too human death drive, without, however, repressing or denying it.

I never thought that the principal enemy was patriarchy, but I have and still do think that the principal adversary is filiarchy. The coming together of sons and brothers after the regicide to establish democracy radically and a priori excludes women. Society is doubly *hommosexuée*, its emblem of power is no longer mere gold. The Phallus may turn out to be an even more destructive standard. That was the challenge our Movement wanted to take up.

LE DÉBAT : Have subsequent events confirmed this diagnosis ?

ANTOINETTE FOUQUE : Absolutely. And worse than I feared. The project of the brothers has been strengthened. Though forestalled for a time by the Women's Movement, thanks to socialist unity which played a pivotal role, they were quick to take their revenge and the reprisals are far from over. With May '68, we entered into the pre-genital stage. That narcissistic era is very important, both because it holds the promise of progress, of a civilization that privileges the image, and it is part and parcel with the media age ; and because it represents a mortal danger if it is abused through isolation or massive identification. The image reigns supreme. Lacan's « The Mirror Stage »[*Ecrits* 1-7], which he wrote in 1936, foresaw this. In 1968, we shifted into a new libidinal structure that Freud, fifty years earlier, had introduced as narcissism. After the age of passions and interests which Hirschman has written about, now comes the age of powers, of identities, of sovereignties, the age of the narcissistic democratization of absolute monarchy : first the Sun King and then star wars, which Roberto Rossellini's *The Rise to Power of Louis XIV* heralded in so subtle a way. This is the age of the « self-s » : beings who self-produce, self-exhibit, and self-promote like so many self-made goods. We are going to be living through years of pomp and ceremonial, the staging of the ego, a generalized false-self rather than self-building.

Activities that up until now have been done the most discreetly, from mountain-climbing to writing, now have to be exhibited and shown on television. For the last fifteen years any writer short on fame has had to turn around a heliocentric master-word and get up on stage where the ideal substitute for any standard whatsoever draws off of those with the ambition of shining when their turn comes. There is no hint of hegemonic ambition in the personality of Bernard Pivot, in spite of the accusations of this or that wounded Narcissus, but nonetheless, an important part of his fame unquestionably is pure signifying effect.[12]

LE DÉBAT : You have a somber, if not pessimistic, view of what the future holds for us.

ANTOINETTE FOUQUE : In fact, I think that the twenty-first century world of images and sons that lies ahead of us will be one that excludes women and all differences, even as integration will be the only thing anyone will talk about. After all, wasn't the nineteenth century for all its promotion of equality nevertheless the century of the bitterest class struggles ?

LE DÉBAT : Didn't Freud by translating a common prejudice into the language of psychoanalysis, make women the locus of narcissism ?

ANTOINETTE FOUQUE : Yes, but wrongly, in my opinion... That was simply because Freud did not know that a woman could be anything other than either the son's mother, phallicized by her offspring, or else the father's daughter, « the phallus as girl ». Devereux goes even further : speaking of Baubo, he claims that by showing her sex, she immediately situates it on the side of the phallus[13]. Thus with the woman, whatever is not kept hidden is to be considered as something exhibited, as a citizen of the land of the phallus, a naturalized Narcissus. The only thing left for women to do if they want to avoid phallic exhibition is to put on the chador, the ritual foreskin of this « phallic age » from which it is clearly impossible to escape. So we go from Charybdis to Scylla.

But that's a question about which much more needs to be said than I can say here.

Le Débat : In concrete terms, today's proliferation of the image is associated with a transformation of the image of men, a transformation that is generally interpreted as a feminization.

Antoinette Fouque : Masculine and feminine are twins in a way, monozygotic twins who admire each other, trade places with each other in a perverse mode and play on gender, without real sexual intercourse. Femininity is a disguise. Homosexual men, fashion designers, for example, dream of an ideal femininity and project themselves onto it. Along with the feminization you mention, this is the very heart of a false sexual difference that is so constricting for so many women : one has to look like a man dressing up as a woman. We have not gotten out of the category of the double : A and A' rather than A and B.

Le Débat : Could you expand more specifically on the connection you make between « phallic » and « narcissistic » ?

ANTOINETTE FOUQUE : At this stage of an erotics that is very remote from its phallic economy, the nature of showing, of exhibition, of the subject's complacency before the mirror, of the body's syncope, it's hard to distinguish at this stage between the phallus — a stand-in for every visual object of desire — and the representation of an erect penis. As with capitalism, what we're dealing with is a primitive phallicism, a kind of obscene priapism, an apt figure for extremism. Where there are no women, they are put on display ; where there are women, they are prevented from speaking. It's the historical scene of the oldest kind of theater. Women — symptoms of a castration that has nothing to do with them but which the sons resist with all their might because they are victimized by it — are made invisible. There are practically no more women to fill the superstar role of the anchor on the 8 o'clock news. The rallying cry of American therapists and academics is *be visible*. Lacan had already advised his disciples : « Make yourself known ». And so what we are witnessing is the emergence of a new type of person who takes on the task of manufacturing himself through the practice, along with body-building, of what might be called « self-building ». This could well be an obligation that will, as time goes by, become difficult to shirk without succumbing to more and more drastic episodes of manic-depressive delirium.

LE DÉBAT : You are not someone whom one imagines satisfied with merely observing the phenomenon. In the face of this new world, what is there to be done ?

ANTOINETTE FOUQUE : We must be able, through speculation as well as through analytic regression, to get
ahead of what's happening, to fly when we can no
longer limp, because, as usual, history will not speak
in a single voice. Besides, this narcissistic trend
wasn't born yesterday. It corresponds to a perpetual
tendency, but there comes a time when a latent and
diffuse phenomenon manifests itself, takes its place in
history and dominates. That, in particular, I think, is
what May '68 revealed in all its awesomeness, and it is
in this respect that May '68 was a revolution. It need
not be all bad with the historicization of this narcissistic trend that we are facing. This could also very well
be the advent of a higher humanism, of a civilization
in which it might be possible to begin to think. And
while we are at it, we may be able to develop a theory of genitality and think about how to get beyond
self-creationism. The production of life is tripartite :
one multiplied by one makes one. That tripartition is
denatured by the Trinity : One alone in three, three
that make only One. If we succeed in dismantling
such devices, if one day we learn what makes them
exclude every heterogeneity, we will then be able to
think through genitality, to have done with the fantasy of the dark continent. A well-tempered narcissism
must be invented. It's possible to contain the star-cancer of phallic erotics — by star-cancer I mean the flip-
side of disaster — the narcissistic inflation as well as
the ossified phallic disposition that overcompensates
for it, by putting the libidinal economy of the phallus
to work, and by creating the epistemological field of a
libidinal economy specific to women. It is in this way
that we will begin to conceive of a sexually heterogeneous civilization. There are two sexes. It is a reality

that the history of human rights, if it wants to remain worthy of its ideals, should make its fourth principle, after liberty, equality, and fraternity. The Women's Movement has brought with it, from the beginning, this fourth revolution that I used to call the revolution of the symbolic.

It's possible to imagine the creation of an epistemological field that will take its place alongside the social sciences, the sciences of men : it would be the sciences of women, which would proceed from gyneconomy to the articulation of a body of specific rights. The Women's Movement has been and remains one of the most powerfully federative movements of civilization. It is that federative aspect which makes me prefer the expression « movement of civilization » to « social movement ». It is in the process of unfolding throughout the world. It's a transnational rather than an international movement — it raises specific problems in each country but the principles are universal and general. Women's political choices are thus registered at the planetary level. It is within such a framework that we must come to terms with a modern conception of women's rights, of the status of women and their demands for identity. With this should come solutions to some of the major problems that presently threaten democracy.

First of all, there are the great problems of the East, the South, and the Maghreb — nationalisms, fundamentalisms but also religious archaisms and traditionalist stereotypes. I could speak once again of the return of the sons : Isaac, Ishmael, Œdipus, Jesus, all of them figures of a narcissistic fundamentalism, of a symbolic stereotype. In the rise of fraternity, in the fratricidal duels, partition or rupture still too often takes place via the bodies of women which become the symptoms through which the madness and the depressive megalomania of the sons is expressed. In India, Moslem women are taking a stand against the enactment of laws regulating personal behavior, against the *charia*, and they are aligning themselves with women in the secular and democratic Indian state. In Algeria, women are mobilizing around the same principles and against the same oppression. Sometimes even risking their lives in the process, they are going to advance not just their own demands but also the cause of Algerian democracy in general.

And then there are the problems of inequality in the work force, of so-called unemployment, of a two-or three-speed European society, all problems that concern women directly. Unequal employment is compounded by unequal visibility. In this society, the dominant males appropriate for their exclusive enjoyment not only the creative work but the gold, the power, and the airwaves and movie screens. There is not a single woman among those « at the helm », not a single woman among the thinkers who claim to be leading the century. Narcissism at the end of the twentieth century no longer has anything to do with the flower or the poem. We have not only to share the labor but also to give value to and recognize new kinds of production. By taking into account the kinds of production that are specifically those of women, the value of new tasks will be recognized, and a better balance of power will be achieved. Of course I have in mind women's creation of children. Today, knowledge of the fertility process is bringing to light the dissymmetry between the sexes in the matter of procreation, a dissymmetry in women's favor. This gap, this inequality with respect to biological roles, this procreative power henceforth can overturn the order of inequalities and transform itself into demographic power. Between 1975 and 1988, there was a one hundred percent increase in the number of single mothers.

Finally, only permanent democratization can guarantee the expansion of democracy. Along with the social contract, today we can speak of a contract with nature and of a contract with life. It's a question not only of protecting what is human but of choosing one's identity, one's life. That's the question of any integration that is harmonized with the power to decide.

And along with rights, we have desires and duties. Women will have to overcome their repugnance and their inhibitions with respect to power. They will have to agree to assume responsibility, to consider that they have a right to be present and a duty to democratize the polis. The *Alliance des Femmes pour la Démocratisation* [Women's Alliance for Democratization][14] would like to encourage and promote further thought and new commitments in these directions.

Translator's
NOTES

1. Or « to talk twaddle. » Literally, *déconner* is « to uncunt ».

2. The publishing house that brought out the works of France's intellectual avant-garde (Lacan, Barthes, Derrida...). The journal of literary ans social theory *Tel Quel* was also published by Le Seuil.

3. *Ecole Normale Supérieure* or, *Normale Sup'*, was created at the end of the 19th century as an elite state school of higher education, specializing in the training of future academics and scho-

lars. The school is comprised of two divisions, one for men and one for women. The famous one is the male branch, located rue d'Ulm in Paris.

4. An avant-garde, socially progressive branch of University of Paris, ParisVIII-Vincennes, now located at Saint-Denis, was founded in 1969 as a concession to the demands of the 68' revolutionaries.

5. *Les femmes s'entêtent* puns with *les femmes sans tête,* or « headless, that is to say, leaderless women ».

6. The *Ecole freudienne* was founded by Lacan in 1965 and dissolved by him in 1984, shortly before he died.

7. In 1971, as a protest against the criminalization of abortion, 343 women, including a number of celebrities, signed a petition declaring that they had had an abortion. The petition appeared in the national press.

8. The law which authorized abortion in 1975 bears the name of Simone Veil — Health minister in the Giscard d'Estaing administration — who defended the law before the French government.

9. A widely influential French marxist and philosopher, Louis Althusser strangled his wife.

10. An autodidact interested in psychoanalysis issues, Daniel Karlin produced and co-hosted with Tony Lainé a weekly television show about the sex lives of the French, entiteled *L'amour en France.* It aired during the 1988-89 season. Antoinette Fouque is referring to the occasion when he stated his fantasmatic identification with a man who had killed his (female) lover.

11. A terrorist group, founded in the early 70s, similar to other European commandos (the Italian Red Brigades, the German Red Army Faction...) who claim affiliation to the extreme left.

12. Bernard Pivot was the creator and host of the influential literary television program, *Apostrophes*, which ran from the late 70s until 1990. Antoinette Fouque plays on his surname to comment on his pivotal role.

13. Georges Devereux, French ethno-psychanalyst.

14. The Alliance is a nonprofit cultural/political organization established by Antoinette Fouque in 1989 (cf. Document p.92).

2

THERE ARE TWO SEXES,
THERE ARE TWO LIBIDOS *

translated by Anne Berger

Passages : What is your personal contribution to psychoanalysis ?

Antoinette Fouque : My contribution is the insistence with which I ask certain questions of psychoanalytical theory ; questions which of course carry within themselves elements of responses. For example, why does the only « scientific » discourse on sexuality, namely the psychoanalytic discourse, assert, from Freud to Lacan, that their is only one libido and that it is of the « male essence » or « phallic », when clearly there are two sexes in reality ? Could it be that this phallic monism, contaminated by the « vir » even more than analysts themselves wish to consider — the phallus being quite often confused, even within theory itself, with the penis — obeys more the

---

* An interview by Emile Malet in the French review *Passages* n°37, Avril-Mai 1991, in the special dossier : « Does psychoanalysis have all the answers ? »

principle of pleasure than that of reality ? Thus, what is referred to as the symbolic order could well be founded on a denial of reality : only one libido, male, for both men and women ! This monophallicism cannot help but evoke monotheisms. Might psychoanalytic theory then originate more in a religious model than a scientific one ?

This produces all sorts of consequences, not to speak of perverse effects. For example it becomes impossible to describe women's sexuality as other than gelded — negative phallicity —, or to designate it as feminine, whereas femininity is a quality also attributable to men. I have long wanted to say that femininity is a travestite, and that in any case, Freud rightly connotes it as passive, referring it back to the anal register of sexuality ; therefore pregenital.

Encysted thus in pregenitality, for men also, which I will come back to, psychoanalytic theory is stuck in a regredient (retrogressive) attraction of the phallic for the anal, in a perverse phallic fixation, which strongly forbids it from elaborating a genital theory since genitality is necessarily heterosexed.

Another perverse consequence : hysterical neurosis is the obverse of phallic perversion. But, if the master's discourse is enlightened by the regression of the discourse of the hysteric — hysteria being the lease the phallus takes on the uterus — why wouldn't it be further enlightened by women's discourse ? Submitting to the principle of reality should make the psychoanalytic discourse progress by permitting it to elaborate a theory of genitality, which could only be as we know, heterosexed. Strangely enough women psychoanalysts who work with or through their women analysees on a sexuality in common continue to affirm theoretically this « only » [« there is only one libido » and « the only joy is that of the phallus »]. Is this so as to not risk losing the love of the father, or a place in this or that institutional house ?

The right of women to the symbolic, that is the right of men and women to a « dialogical order », might allow us to understand what the sexual relation is, or is not, about. But this right of women to the symbolic demands that we consider that just as there are two sexes, there are two libidos and that each woman has her own libido. Some 20 years ago I called it « libido 2 », but after all, since it is a uterine libido with a matrical economy, it could just as well be called, being primary, the first and fundamental for both sexes, « libido 1 » !

PASSAGES : Are you saying that psychoanalysis is a science of man ?

ANTOINETTE FOUQUE : Theory, or rather psychoanalytic discourse was in fact elaborated by a man, Freud, « vir » and « homo sapiens » at the same time, based on the words of young women qualified as hysteric ; but, Freud the writer has in part repressed the women subject from her own words. Though he started from *Studies on Hysteria* and then conjugated dreams and hysteria in « Dora », Freud finally gave as the royal road of the unconscious *The Interpretation of Dreams*, where he took himself most often as the object of study making his own obsessional masculine neurosis the foundation of psychoanalytic knowledge.

The repression of hysteria, traceable to the foreclo- sure of the uterus, can be seen in more than one place in Freud's works. Freud himself recognized that he wasn't able to take into account Dora's homo-

sexuality, and that he was mistaken in his interpretation of transference : elsewhere in his analysis of the
poetess Hilda Doolittle, he refused to assume the
maternal role in the counter-transference. We know
today that he worked very little on his relationship to
his mother in his self-analysis, and that in the definitive edition of his notes on « The Rat Man » , he massi-
vely repressed maternal references; so that finally his
desire of the matrical even if it does appear in one of
the key dreams of the *Interpretation*... , that of « anatomical representation », gives no grounds for any elaboration of his uterine impulse, his female being,
other than in a cryptic metaphor. Indeed, if repression is one of the fundamental concepts of psychoanalysis, even perhaps its keystone, the foreclosure of
the mother's body, as that of the name of the father
conceptualized by Lacan, is also capable of generating
psychosis : what is foreclosed from the symbolic
makes its return in the real.

Bordering beneath and beyond the phallic-anal problematic, which occupies practically the entire field
of psychoanalytic theory, women's sexuality could be
elaborated from an articulation of the oral-genital.
The writer predator of the talking cure invented by
Anna O. died of mouth cancer which reduced him to
mutism at the end of his life ; he had intended to
construct a theory of orality ; this project aborted
perhaps because work on the prenatal, on pregnancy,
on the sexual body, on the thinking flesh of women
as a producer of living-speaking, had been foreclosed
from the science of the unconscious. If I dared I
would say that the epistemophillic impulse had dege-
nerated in order to write itself into an epistemophal-
lic impulse, at the expense of an analytic and concep-

tual advance, where the son would be emancipated geni(t)ally (*géni(t)alement* — with genius) from the fantasy of an all-powerful mother. For sons pay dearly for their desire to be loved without ambivalence, to want to be taken for God, and stay thus riveted to Her, from fathers to sons, rather than recognizing that they are simply born of women and that like them they are human beings, neither more nor less, though sometimes of genius.

Perhaps mono-phallo-theism was a spiritual progress, but at the price of such misogyny that it would appear more and more to be an agent of sclerosis, a perverse fixation, and an impoverishment for humanity. The vital link to the matrical, foreclosed from the symbolic, makes its return in the real as a dependence on the archaic mother, and misogyny, a fear and hatred felt by men towards women that voids the human contract.

PASSAGES : What is then, according to you, the work to be done in psychoanalysis to get out of this deadend ?

ANTOINETTE FOUQUE : It is urgent to secularize and democratize psychoanalytic theory, which means not only making a place for the mother in the house of the father, but also freeing ourselves from pre-genital and infantile dependence. Far from wanting to destroy the body of Freudian construction, admirable in its foundation and achievement from the cellar to the attic, certain aspects should be restored ; it should be enlarged with some indispensable supplementary rooms. As regards genealogies, birth certificates, proper names and family ties, it is time to reconsider the matrical function, the maternal responsibility, the place of the woman-subject in this house ; in one word, to rethink the post-patriarchal, so as to invent ourselves as either men or women, but together.

The work to be done then is the anamnesis of the relation to this unknown, the elaboration of this vital link to the matrical. To go beyond envy, to recognize the capacity to dream of the mother, as does Bion, or better, to recognize the impulse to know, the capacity of welcoming the other of a woman, is to attain gratitude, it is already to approach what we could call thinking. It is perhaps to begin to move from a mode of religious or too often obscurantist thinking, to a mode of thinking that is scientific and ethical.

The symbolizable experience, virtual or real, of pregnancy is experienced by each woman as the intimate labor of self and non-self. It is the model for all successful grafting of a « thinking of the other », of a heterogeneous « between us », of the tolerance of another's pleasure, of hospitality towards a stranger's body, of a gift without indebtedness, of love for your neighbor, of a promise to keep, of a carnal hope that disavows all absolute narcissism, all totalitarian one-dividualism, all racism. Those specific capacities can be transmitted and shared in the co-creation man-woman which is human procreation.

It is time to be done with misogyny, it is time that knowledge and the gratitude of thinking attempt to triumph over the relation to the unknown ; the envy and obscurantism shown towards women. It is time to be done with the fantasy of the « dark continent ».

A woman's ethic would join with, by having inspired it, that of the thinker poets, Rimbaud, Rilke...

Let us remind ourselves of that phrase pronounced by Paul Celan in his *Bremen Discourse* : « To think (*denken*) and to thank (*danken*) have in our language one and the same origin. Whosoever abandons themselves to their senses is adventuring into the signifying field of living memory (*gedenken*), reminding (*eingedenk sein*), Remembrance (*Andenken*), Gathering (*Andacht*). Permit me to thank you from such a field ».

3

THE REPUBLIC OF SONS *

translated by ANNE BERGER

At Epinay, in 1971, on the heels of the « '68 revolution », Francois Mitterrand democratized the paternalistic SFIO[1] by creating a modern Socialist Party (PS), a more reasonable older brother to the sons in revolt, a party capable of destroying in the medium term the Gaullian authoritarianism which was to mark France for still another decade by anchoring it on the right.

In 1981 then, the Father on the left and the Father on the right would be definitively evicted. This mitterrandian victory, contrary to appearances, would mark the transformation of the notable efforts at the end of the 60's by the left-third world-isms, rather than the accomplishment of the socialist-communist dream. All the deceptions and surprises of the last 10 years are witness.

In May 68, with the œdipian anti-authoritarian crisis, the era of the all powerful photoscopic begins. It is the passing of the post-monarchical industrial era, the

---

* Appeared in *Passages* n°38, May 1991, in the special dossier : « Mitterrand and the iniquities. »

era of interest, of capitalism, the era of the man-father, the bourgeois, and his other, the proletarian, the man of the worker's movement, of the socialist counter-power, and the beginning of the pre-democratic era of communication, the era of the power of identity and phallicism, the era of the man-son and narcissism ; from hands on to on-looker ; the man-star, mutant anti-œdipus or Priapus, the Prince, the first, the impressive (*primé*), which entails its obverse, the depressive (deprimed/*déprimé*) ; but both participating in the same structural envy, the same creative anguish. Succeeding to the Leninist « What is to be done ? » is the arrivist « How to do it ? » The 19th century and the era of liberty-equality are done with; the 21st century and the era of « liberty-fraternity » has begun.

The democratic revolution is the foundation of a fraternal and fratricidal filocracy, the beginning of a fratriarchy ˙; it repeats, in a lay mode, the christian dissidence that founded our era.

Where once was the religion of the Father the religion of the Son has been installed ; where once was was the Republic of the Fathers, advances the Republic of the Sons. From May '68 to May '91, from the graffiti on the walls of the Sorbonne (« power is at the end of the phallus ») to the tags at the Louvre subway station, from « Nique Ta Mère » (« Screw your mother »), a group of suburban rappers, to N.T.M. superstars of clubs and music video, in time and in space the liberation process, œdipalization, democratization of the sons therefore, continues under the guidance of Francois Mitterrand. Nevertheless we are still far from the transformation of a phallic erotic into an œdipal economy. And once again, homosexed (sic)

---

* Cf. « Women in movements, yesterday, today, tomorrow. », p.37.

as in the ancient athenian model, democracy has a tendency to construct itself without women, and they who have so largely contributed to the victory of the left are again left to ask themselves how they can exist in this Republic of Sons.

On March 8, 1981, the *Mouvement de Libération des Femmes* (Women's Liberation Movement) called for a first round vote for Francois Mitterrand, and on May 10, 1981, for the first time since the right to vote was granted them, the majority of women voted for the left. In 1986 however their hearts leaned anew to the the right, and if you can believe in a recent poll, there are today fewer women than men who approve of Francois Mitterrand.

Ever since May '68 there have been a few of us who have participated in this great upheaval. In '70 we were thousands, in '79, tens of thousands. All of us demanded the freedom to dispose of our own bodies and the acknowledgement of our existence in history. Our movement was cultural and symbolic as well as economic and social ; our project was global, world-wide, and not reducible to any one priority [abortion, rape] fetishized by the medias.

Some among us, as an echo to the narcissistic revolution, have chosen to take the way of equality, the logic of identity : from now on, the one is the other since tomorrow legally the other equals the one. To be « daughter » to the father, younger sister of the older brother, feminist at the side of the leftist, Trotskyist, communist, socialist or anarchist seemed satisfactory or in any case felt secure. The reward for this fraternization with the son's law was rapid but of short duration in the light of History. After the creation of a sub-ministry for the feminine condition by

ANTOINETTE FOUQUE

Valery Giscard d'Estaing and the zenith of what must be called a state feminism with, in '81, a ministry of women's rights, we have rapidly returned to sub-ministeries without any real autonomy; the present sub-ministry had to be wrenched in high combat by a thousand feminist petitioners from the second government of Michel Rocard (the Prime Minister had at first declared that he didn't want, for women, a ghetto ministry).

The 80's were dominated by anti-racist movements faced with the National Front (FN) [2] and fundamenta-lisms ; fraternity and fratricide : « Don't touch my buddy »[3], « Don't touch my novel » (S. Rushdie), but unfortunately also, « Don't touch my flag », « Don't touch my Koran ». Are the Algerian FIS (Islamic Fundamentalist Party) [4] and the National Front only extreme caricatures of The Republic of Sons, the per-verse effects of democratization ? Fundamentalisms also secrete their own feminism. In Europe the ecolo-gists have created the first party of protectors-sons of mother-nature. In Poland, the new democrats, adorers of the Virgin, penalize abortion.

At any rate, in the 80's fraternity advances ; exit the women's movement. As if a man can only tolerate one other at a time, the woman or the brother. And when it's the brother, we women are all thrown back to the ancient destiny of Iphigenia, Jocasta, or Antigone.

The medias in their balance for this decade have definitively buried the question of the integration of women, by merging it with chapters of contempora-ry history judged altogether more important by men : nurses have migrated to the chapter on econo-my, muslim women to internal exclusion in the chap-ter on religion.

After all, in effect, we are only a minority, not even 53% of the population. And most of us assume only three modes of « production » ; the human production of the living-speaking (procreation, demographics) ; domestic production (household work, nursing, puericulture, etc.) ; and, professional production. The first two being « slaves », it is normal that those of us in the third category are penalized and underpaid.

There is nonetheless material for a vast reaccounting after 23 years of struggle, and 17 years of State feminism. These ten years are marked, in fact, by restrictions on our power to act, and a rampant contesting of acquired rights, from the right to abortion to the right to work, as if the reigning unemployment had imposed a threshold of tolerance on the women immigrants from the interior.

Without wanting to be exhaustive here and lash out with statistics, it must nevertheless be realized that the National Assembly is composed of 5.7% women, and that only 5.43% of mayors are women, that the unemployment numbers for women (13%) is two times greater than that for men, and that their average salary is inferior by 35%. A law mandating professional equality was voted in 1983, but it was inadequate due to lack of enforcement and the lasting unemployment which burdens women especially. Thus, access to economic power remains blocked. The quota law, which would have increased women's access to political power, was declared invalid by the Constitutional Council [5] where not one woman sits. And worse, the proposal for an anti-sexist law which would have permitted women access to symbolic power, and was indispensable for compliance with the « Convention of the United Nations on the elimination of all forms of discrimination as regards women », this legislative proposal put before the National Assembly had to be withdrawn by the government under pressure from the media.

And meanwhile we have not ceased to affirm our own identity, to struggle for our right to Rights and to fight against misogyny which from now on can be considered a « crime against humanity ».

Each year in France two million women are battered, more than four thousand women are raped ; and every day a misogynist crime is committed, most often accompanied by rape and torture. A society that was able to abolish the death penalty must commit itself to fight by all possible means against the specific barbarism of misogyny. The future Penal code, and Book II particularly, must fill this legislative gap so as to demonstrate to the international community the will of French society to defend Men's human rights against savagery, in strict conformity not only with the « Convention of the United Nations against torture » but also with « the United Nations Convention against all forms of discrimination against women » (1980). (On March 8, 1990, the United Nations explicitly affirmed that there is no truly developed country in the world for women.) The reform of the Penal code undertaken by G. Kiejman [6] goes in the right direction by specifying the treatment and suppression of « barbaric crimes » and « crimes against humanity », and by reinforcing the means of defense of the « most vulnerable ».

If Amnesty International has recently inscribed sexual difference in its international statutes, on the other hand, the preamble of our Constitution of 1958 following the lead of the 1946 Constitution grants the citizens of this country « an inalienable and sacred right, without distinction of race, religion or belief », while forgetting sex ; we ought from now on be able to read that all citizens, both men and women, of our country have « an inalienable and sacred right regardless of sex, ethnic background, religion, or beliefs ». It is time to grant women the right to Rights.

Already in 1968 some women chose the way of difference rather than equality, working so that women could succeed where hysteria and its dream of a bi-sexed symmetry had failed. They wanted to bring about a movement counter-powering identity in resistance to ancient and new misogynies, patriarchal and filiarcal ; to invent a liberation movement, followed by democratization, post-phallic, post-Œdipal, by virtue of which women would need no longer to be sisters or mothers to be « screwed ». They were of the opinion that there could be no justice without accurate analysis ; that democratic equal rights would remain a mirage, enslaved to the culturalistic pleasure principle if the reality of sexual difference is denied, and that otherwise this unsymmetry would remain after the elimination of all forms of discrimination. Difference without equality is a reactionary archaism, equality without working on differences is a sterile illusion. If in the 70's, ideologies and their « isms » have repressed analytical thinking, and if, in the 80's, rights have inhibited politics, starting today, starting tomorrow, together with thought and action both psychoanalytical and political, ideologies could represent the virtues of the creative imagination and the law could be the most reliable auxiliary to long term policy, a time of fecundity.

Some men would have us believe that the women's movement is obsolete, even dead, that women's struggles are behind us, when they have only just begun ; they take their mysogynistic desires for reality.

French women, French men, one more effort if we want to be democratic. What has been accomplished is not negligible, but almost everything remains to be done. Tomorrow the young will be old, the Whites and the Blacks will be coffee and cream colored (*café au lait*), but tomorrow women will still be women.

As hope is not necessary to endeavor, nor success to perseverance, so unanimity is not a requisite for continuing. Sometimes the approval of only one can be sufficient. The president of the Republic has personally on several occasions firmly encouraged me to continue. « Continue », it's his word. And coming from a man who has not known how to stop, who continues to labor, it is like a rendezvous made for 10 years later, for 20 years later, and more, with our History. It is an incitement to progress, to democratization, to make France advance from a Republic of Sons to a Republic of men and women.

NOTES

1. SFIO, *Section française de la IIe Internationale Ouvrière*, French Section of the Second Workers International, founded in 1905, forerunner of the Socialist Party.

2. French extreme-right wing party.

3. « Don't touch my buddy » is the famous slogan of the SOS Racism, the anti-racist organization founded and led by Harlem Desir.

4. In French, FIS is a homonym of the word for son « fils ».

5. The Constitutional Council is responsible for ensuring the constitutionality of France's laws and international obligations.

6. Georges Kiejman : lawyer, former Minister with special responsability for Justice, Communication, currently for Foreign Affairs.

4

AND IF WE SPOKE OF
THE IMPOWER OF WOMEN ? *

translated by Nina Mc Pherson

To speak of the power of women in France, where their presence in positions of political power is so negligible, would be almost laughable. The statistics are quite damning ; France very nearly brings up the rear in this particular domain[1]. Moreover, just as a single swallow does not make a summer, the presence of a woman as French Prime Minister, despite the indisputable symbolic effect of this presidential initiative, does not represent a rapid transformation of reality. In fact, there are no more women in Edith Cresson's government now than there were in that of her predecessor, Michel Rocard. More importantly, the current French government has made no real attempt to strengthen its policy towards women, with the exception of the reestablishment of a ministry solely dedicated to women, as in 1981.

_____

* Appeared in *Passages* n°40, septembre 1991, in the special dossier : « Do women like power ? »

Today, almost a quarter of a century after the democratic revolution of 1968 and the organization of the
women's movement, women's access to the ranks of
political, economic, and symbolic power, remains difficult, not to say impossible. This is the case, despite
women's partially acquired access to knowledge — at
least in the West — and which does not represent a
concomitant access to "worth".[2]

Don't women like power ? Or is it power that
doesn't like them ?

Women are segregated, more often than not, with
their special problems, and when it comes to conside-
ring great options for the future, it is assumed that
they have no opinion on these questions. They forget
to ask. The newspaper, « Seen From The Left » edited
by Jean Poperen, is remarkable in this sense. But we
could come up with infinite examples in the media.
Do women actually like power ? It's like asking if
poor people like money... No, because they don't
have any ; yes, because they don't have any.

In this rather dreary political summer, two news
events or issues which concern women have caused a
few waves in the murky backwaters of the media, the
trade unions and French politics ; the third, the most
serious, is not an issue but a tragedy : I refer to the
rape of 71 young women and the murder of 19 of
these women at a highschool in Kenya by their own
male classmates, an event which apparently only
barely received press coverage. Here in France, the
only media attention given to the rapes and violences
against women has taken the form of the obligatory
coverage of their assassins. [3]

The first question, then, is a study conducted by the
« Horizon 2000 » of INSEE (The French National

AND IF WE SPOKE OF THE IMPOWER OF WOMEN ?

Insitute of Economic and Statistical Information), which predicts a shortage of manpower in 2005. INSEE's logic is as follows: if the fertility rate remains at its current level, the population which they call « active », will diminish. To remedy this situation, they propose four solutions : increasing the productivity of the population, extending the duration of its activity, increasing employment opportunities for women or relaunching immigration policies. Virtually everyone seized upon the fourth solutio : for the political Left, it served their predictions of a good immigration in the year 2000, and for the Right and the Extreme Right, it helped unmask the motivation behind the study : a policy in support of a rising birth rate. The conclusion took the form of two simultaneous and inextricably linked exclusions : the exclusion of immigrants, so threatening today and in the future, that we must rush to close the borders ; and the exclusion of women, who while destined to reproduce French manpower, are considered « inactive ». In the future, these women will not even hold the lead in the category of the long-term unemployed that they are today. Women constitute 57 percent of long-term unemployed, and young women 76 percent of young long-term unemployed — an unemployment which marginalizes them economically, politically, and socially.

The mobilization of society's resources for a policy which would recognize women as triply productive members of society should be a priority for the political Left. In reality, the Left has forgotten women and made them the most excluded category in this competitive and production-oriented society. And this has occurred despite the fact that women are, in fact, triply productive in human society — as reproducers

65

who have the exclusive task of perpetuating the species, as productive housewives responsible for the family or private sphere, and finally, and in large numbers, as working professionals whose activities are now indispensable for the maintenance of a barely decent standard of living. But as a result of their multiple duties, women find themselves the majority in a legion of long-term unemployed ; in other words, they find themselves the most excluded of the excluded in this competitive society.

Moreover, the « inactive » and « active » categories which demographers apply to us not only make the female population a divided people, arbitrarily separated by social affiliations and diverse cultures, but also make each individual woman, each one of us, into a person torn between her need for intimate accomplishment and her desire for legitimate social ambition.

The fertility rate is the blind spot around which this type of demography is organized, this human pseudo-science, so surreal in its attempt to saw off the very branch on which it sits that it excludes women from its analyses, the very life source of its legitimacy. In effect, if demography does not consider reproducing women part of the active population, then, how will an active manpower be born of such an inactive source ? And how will future generations renew themselves other than through the reproductive capacity of the female population, which while counted as « inactive » constitutes the very core of the active population, generation after generation. In other terms, humanity, as Lacan once put it, would be a woman who makes a woman who makes a woman, one after the other, inactive according to the demographers, but always present as a factory reserved for the sole use of the active population. When we speak of electric or atomic energy, we consider these installations in the cost of production. Human reproduction, however, is left out of the calculation of human productivity and the resources that it creates : certainly this omission is the last, but most formidable, pocket of slavery.

Despite this reality, not a single journalist, not a single policy has noted, in commenting on the INSEE study, the polemic unleashed last spring surrounding the question of fertility indexes : 1.8 or 2.1. At the time, people spoke of an infiltration of the INED by the right wing National Front. [4]

The capacity to reproduce, this specific power of women, instead of engendering power (some speak of demographic power), has shackled us to a very real impower, precisely because human reproduction is so negatively inscribed in democratic thought, which while understandably concerned with its principles of equality, is oblivious to the reality and the dissymmetry between the two sexes, when it comes to this principle difference. And, as we know from psychoanalysis, that which is symbolically repressed returns in reality ; that which reality refuses to consciously think will resurface as a symptom at each step of the way in our progress towards democratization. In virtually all their activities, women are penalized for their reproductive power, an activity which is qualified as inactive.

Even to speak of reproduction, of maternity, often appears to be a regressive and reactionary attitude in and of itself — mainly because, up until now, only the political Right wing speaks of it, and when they speak of it in the context of their programme for an accele-

67

rated birth rate, they exacerbate this penalization. As a result, the Women's Movement has always stood on the political Left, has always put nurture before nature (the reverse of the Environmental Movement) and has always considered reproduction to be a choice, a culturally rather than biologically determined fact of life, which a woman's mastery of fertility would humanize even further. To have proposed a greater articulation between the private and the public spheres is not the least of the advances made by the Women's Movement ; there is the distinction between the subject and history, the rethinking of the body as both capable of suffering and joy, more than just a mere vehicle for work ; there is also the appearance of the subject as political, a topic forgotten by Marx, either embryonic or already born. Once qualified as a social movement, the Women's Movement has always defined itself as a cultural and civilizing movement with a universal mission.

Whether women are referred to as producers or reproducers, they are the source of the principal human resource : humanity itself. The demographers should not only speak of the « active population », but also of ingenious brains and creative intelligences. Reproduction remains excluded — and I will say it again — from the productivity-oriented thought which it feeds and which defines it as an impower.

The second current event confirms this analysis. The European Court of Justice recently lifted the ban on night work for women in the name of the equality of the sexes. On the side of the workers, those archaic dreamers, we heard cries of regression : we must eliminate night work for both sexes ; from the managers, we heard cries of progress : women are achie-

ving and being promoted as fast as their male coun-
terparts, except in the « special case of maternity »
(These were the terms used in the declaration by the
the General Confederation of Cades trade union !).
Affirmative action for women is inscribed in the
French labor law and is a protection against sexual
abuse and the financial burden of raising a family. But
as far as I know, rapes and violent acts against women
have not diminished in our country. Moreover, if one
is to believe INSEE, the fertility rate per woman is 1.8
(or 2.1 for the INED, the National Institute of
Demographic Studies), which means that every non-
pubescent and non-menopausal woman in this country is potentially responsible for producing two children, and this is true for 53 percent of the population. Is maternity then a « special case » or more general one, the case of the majority of women ?

We cannot simultaneously credit each woman with a
fertility rate — thus holding her body responsible for
the renewal or the ageing of the species and blaming
her for any demographic imbalances — and continue
to consider pregnancy or maternity as a « special
case ». These concepts of fertility rates and demographic equilibrium make reproduction a general destiny
and force a solidarity between women which requires
that reproduction become a universal concept inte-
grated into democratic ideals.

No doubt it will be argued that there are very
sophisticated machines which work non-stop, day
and night. But let us at least organize three eight hour
shifts instead of these new automotons. However, a
qualified woman technician (many women already
are these days and will be in even greater numbers
tomorrow), the mother of a three-year old child who

is pregnant with a second, could never, under any circumstances, imagine coping with the three eight hour shifts during a pregnancy which mobilizes a huge expense of her energy on a 24-hour basis. But in the name of equality, we will make her work the night shift, and in the name of protective discrimination, or affirmative action, we will then go and penalize her when she seeks promotion. This is a scandal : the egalitarian and production-obsessed ideology which excludes the urgent issue of reproduction from its dynamic, excludes women from the very outset.

In Honduras, 3,000 young girls between the ages of 15 and 20 were forcibly sterilized to satisfy employers who wanted to abolish the maternity leave which they claimed disrupted the organization of their work (Cf. the French version of *Elle*, August 5, 1991). All over the world, women are slaves and martyrs to reproduction ; whether it is forbidden or obligatory, whether it is under totalitarian or egalitarian skies, it is always by a society which is opportunistic and sadistic in its obsession with productivity ; in which women are invisible slaves to a kind of production which has never even been considered by any economic theory as such. Women have been martyrs, since the earliest days of human history, and even today ; martyrs of their exclusive knowledge of the flesh, a knowledge which is often considered diabolical and which has been the object of a « gynocide » by an Inquisition which has burned them by hundreds of thousands.

Today misogyny takes the form of a fanatical, anti-feminism which means that even a women's elementary right to knowledge carries the risk of death. Is it even necessary to recall the Quebec tragedy, replayed in an even more horrific version in the Kenya tragedy ? In Canada, in December 1989, a young man assasinated 14 students at the Montreal Polytechnic in an attack against women who attempt to gain a higher education. In Nairobi, on July 13, 1991, a hord of 300 boys, aged 14 to 19, students in a mixed Catholic school, engaged in a collective massacre of young girls. Drunk and drugged out, armed with iron bars, these boys stormed the girls' dormitory, wounded 75 of these girls, raped 71 of them and killed 19. These girls had preferred to continue studying during an examination period rather than join a strike which they felt did not concern them against the leadership of the school. « Murderous insanity » read the headlines in the newspapers, which only gave a few lines of coverage to the tragedy. Insanity should never, in any case, be considered an attenuating circumstance to justify misogynist and anti-feminist crimes and violence, any more than it should ever be used to justify racial violence or crimes of a racist nature. However, while racism is now considered an offence, misogyny remains an opinion, and sexist murders are written off as the work of madmen, whose madness renders them irresponsible and thus utterly unaccountable.

The task of democratic men and women can be defined on three levels :

First, the struggle to eradicate a deep misogyny which both maintains women in a state of impower and plots their gynocide. The decline of Marxism threatens to bring about a renaissance of a metaphysical philosophy which would make women the first of its victims. A deep reflection on the issue of reproduction should be the first condition for elaborating a system of thought which is not metaphysical. By taking human reproduction into consideration, this thought, far from being a regression, would eliminate more than one deranged type of logic ; it would also finally recognize the social dimension of reproduction, one of the most vital activities of our species — for its genealogy, for its memory, for its transmission and its history.

Secondly, we must struggle through our involvement in anti-establishment structures, taking the side of those who have been excluded from and disinherited by the international competitive and productive system.

Thirdly, and finally, we must struggle to pave the way for women's access to all existing power structures, according to the democratic principles: « in equality and in respect of our differences », and not the inverse. The process of democratization must from now on be inscribed in an egalitarian framework — the existence of the two sexes and their dissymmetry — and it must put women in control of their fertility, not just in terms of its biological fact, but in its full civic and symbolic sense.

NOTES

1 Cf. « The Republic of Sons », p.55.

2 Cf. « The Three Revenges » by Jean-Claude Chesnais in *Le Débat* n°.60, May-August 1990, Gallimard.

3. The press had a field day this summer with crime, turning several women criminals into stars so that at least in this field we might see some equality. A mirage, as always, when it is a question of equality between men and women (Cf. the statistics of the Ministry of Justice on crime in France published by *Le Nouvel Observateur* of June 6-12, 1991 : more than 88 percent of murderers are men.)

4. Cf. May 17, 1990 issue of the *Nouvel Observateur*.

5

WHAT ABOUT
ARAB INTELLECTUAL WOMEN ? *

translated by Nina Mc Pherson

Do they really have women intellectuals, the North
Africans, the Egyptians, the peoples of the Middle
East ? Yes, these women exist, and for more than thirty years, and throughout the course of their history,
we have met many, published a few, read even more
of them. The richness of this talented group of
women is such that we will need more time, more
space, more competence than I have to here to
convey just who they are. What these women are
courageously in the process of achieving merits an
extensive study, rigorous and open-minded.
Undoubtedly it would have been more equitable if
the words of these women had been allowed to fill at
least half of this article. These few lines scrawled in
haste are only an attempt to fill the void; we are wai-
ting for something better.

---

* Appeared in *Passages* n°41, October 1991 in the special dossier :
« Ten Arab Intellectuals look at Israël. »

Essayists, novelists, academics, researchers, poets, philosophers, civil servants, activists — these women are each now firmly grounded in a genealogy which is more than a century old.

At the beginning of this century, one of them was named May Ziyadé, an Egyptian renowned for her writings and her literary « salon » ; she became a pioneering figure ; declared insane, she was locked away in a psychiatric asylum. Not to speak of Aïcha Taymour, Zeynab Fawaz...

From the Second World War to the struggle for independence, they are called, and they call each other : Djamila Debèche who works for the radio and is listened to attentively by all the women who work in the Algerian countryside ; she creates a newspaper, *Action* to defend their rights. Marguerite Taos Amrouche... and Assia Djebar, the third woman novelist ever to be published in Algeria and who was an immediate success. From the 1960s on, in rhythm with national liberation movements, and in reaction to the mounting pressure for Islamic fundamentalism, these women wrote mainly in French and were published, for the most part, in Paris. Our contemporaries from this part of the world, among others, are called : Souad Guellouz, Hélé Béji, Venus Khoury-Ghata, Etel Adnan, Aïcha Lemsine, Leila Sebbar, Fattouma Touati, Fatima Mernissi, Andrée Chedid, Fatima Gallaire, Malika Greffou, Naoual El Saadaoui, Fatiha Hakiki-Talahite, Noria Allami, Nina Bouraoui, Alya Saada... Whether they are sixty years old or twenty-five years old, whether they come from Algeria, Tunisia, Morocco, Egypt, Libya, Iraq or other Arab and Muslim countries, judging from their national destinies and their condition, nothing is strange to their double

WHAT ABOUT THE ARAB INTELLECTUAL WOMEN ?

consciousness as women and as the once-colonized. Standing as they are at the crossroads of two cultures, these women have an exceptional vantage point from which to observe the problems which have arisen from the geographic and cultural contiguity of the Arab and Western-Christian worlds : tensions, contradictions, conflicts, paradoxes, ambiguities, dismemberings, but especially all the possible interlockings, integrations, and enrichments. « I do not feel that there is any conflict between the different contributions of the cultures that I know. No more than East and West, North and South. These cultures are not contradictory for me, they are mutually enriching. » (Naoual El Saadaoui)

In the heat of political struggle, it has become apparent that the participation of these women has always marked a cultural and ethical cape or crossroads between tradition (call it the gratitude of their flesh) and modernity (call it their lucid emancipation to support political independence) : « I carry all these crowds within me. My Algerian mother opened the world to me and with her all the women I have loved, all my mothers. One language which swims in another language and comes out of it enriched. I am not made of two halves. It is a question of adding and creating synergies and connections, flowing together, merging. The advantages of crossbreeding more than compensate for its discomforts... » (Fatima Gallaire).

Even if what all these women have in common is their possession of a dual origin, a dual language, a dual nationality, they never speak in the same voice ; so concerned is each of these women to produce a new and singular analysis of what it means today to be a woman, an intellectual, an Arab — at once doubly

« Other » and yet a full-fledged citizen of the world.

When confronted with all the questions common to Arab intellectuals, from decolonization to the Palestinian cause, caught between the easterly and westerly winds, but confronted — and in this instance it is the most frequently without men — with questions specific to women, these women do not necessarily come up with the same answers. Conscious of the fact that without equity, without parity, without women, there can be no democracy, these women are themselves trying to avoid what Hélé Béji has discovered to be their « Interior Occident ».

But the objective stake or interest these women have in the opening of the Arab world to the West is obvious : « The 21st century is on its way. We cannot isolate ourselves, exclude ourselves. For my part, I refuse the conflict between the Orient and the Occident. We will never advance by defining ourselves in terms of a national identity. » (Malika Greffou).

Very often, the rejection of Islam is not their first priority : « We, women of Arab countries, we know that we are still enduring slavery, but we also know that this kind of slavery is not linked to the fact that we are Orientals or Arabs, or that we are part of Islamic societies, but rather to the fact that the patriarchal system has dominated the world for millenniums. » (Naoual El Saadaoui). The Tunisian, Hélé Béji fervently but rationally calls for secularism : « What ensures that thought will enjoy the guarantee and the richness of its own sovereignty ? Secularism...(It is) the fundamental principle which authorizes this hardy, perennial piece of the inalienable in me, and which, fearless of sanctions by any political or spiritual order, gives me the grace of distance from any political or spiritual constraint. Secularism therefore appears to be the legal basis capable of preserving the right to exercise thought. » But the Algerian Fatiha Hakiki-Talahite remains more pragmatic and prudent : « Today, among Algerian democrats, I see two tendencies. On the one hand, there are those who find the secular political system so convenient, so adapted to modernity, to human rights, to democracy, that they don't see why we shouldn't adopt it. The hitch is that the vast majority of Algerians don't want it (secularism), and you have to be blind not to see that. And this is not only the result of Islamic fundamentalist propaganda — which we have blamed for far too great a share of the impact — but beyond this, the source lies in a reflex which is profoundly rooted in our society, a society which is entering modernity at its own pace, and which has been sufficiently hurried and manhandled along the way to warrant, at least among democrats, the search for a gentler and more flexible mode of transition. »

And if these women do not always argue for the side of Reason and Light, they remain anxious not to exclude the irrational and the unconscious. (Cf. n°1 of the psychology review *Cahiers Intersignes*, « Between Psychoanalysis and Islam », Spring 1990, and *Veiled and Unveiled*, by Noria Allami.)

To the questions posed by the paradoxes of decolonization, the relation between Muslim fundamentalism, the conflict and/or addition of the two languages, the two cultures, the relation to Arab ideologies to modernity, the inside and the outside, the interior exile, to these questions they respond more with words from their bodies, with their reason and their experience, than with the « wooden language » of ideologies and fanaticism.

ANTOINETTE FOUQUE

These women are still far from even having the right
to the protection of any secular Law. Islam is the state
religion in the Republics of Tunisia and Algeria, and in
the Moroccan monarchy where the king is the com-
mander-in-chief of all believers. If the governments of
Egypt, Tunisia, Jordan, Iraq and Yemen have ratified
the United Nations Convention « against all forms of
discrimination towards women », their application of
these principles remains to be verified.

These women stand in solidarity with each other :
« All hope of (national) construction lies with women.
They have no choice and they have nothing to lose.
When they call on me to join them in their activism, I
will do it every time. » (Fatima Gallaire).

These women are wise, even in their violence. « A
message ? Yes. Come out of your lairs, don't waste
our time anymore or theirs. Let us derail the course of
tradition, let us disorient our mores and their values.
Let us rip down all curtains and nets and join our
bodies ! And may a carnival of hands shatter the win-
dows, shatter this silence. » (Nina Bouraoui). Even the
pessimists among them are unyielding: "Culturally, I
am very pessimistic, because of the compromises our
politicians have made with Islamic fundamentalism ;
this has confronted women with great dangers.
Algeria is the most misogynist country in the Arab
world — and that even includes Algerian intellectuals
—- but Algeria is also a country where women are
more organized, a fact that has perhaps permitted
them to progress in other spheres... I support and
stand in solidarity with all the struggles that women
there have led since 1988. » (Assia Djebar). The opti-
mists, the intellectuals among them, contend: « For
the women I am very optimistic. You can see

78

advances being made everywhere. We will see more and more of this in the future, even despite the enormous difficulties... When political power gives them nothing, the women's movement will take to the streets. » (Alya Saada). Their call, today, is a promise which will, inevitably, be kept : « Women will never achieve freedom if they can't manage to organize themselves into a political front which is strong, lucid, and dynamic. If the price of liberty is high, we know from experience that the tribute to the slavery is even higher. » (Naoual El Saadaoui).

BIBLIOGRAPHY

NAOAUL EL SAADAOUI,
Ferdaous, A Voice from Hell,
The Hidden Face of Eve,
Twelve Women of Kanater,
Egyptian Women, Tradition and Modernity
(Des femmes, 1981, 1983, 1984, 1991).

ASSIA DJEBAR
The Thirst, (Julliard, 1957).
The Rebellious, (Julliard, 1958).
The Children Of a New World, (Julliard, 1962).
Women Of Algiers in their homes, (Des femmes, 1980).

HELE BEJI,
The National Disenchantment : An Essay on Decolonization
(La Découverte, 1982).
The Eye of The Day, (M. Nadeau, 1985).

NORIA ALLAMI
Veiled, Unveiled (L'Harmattan, 1988).

NINA BOURAOUI
The Forbidden Voyeur (Gallimard, 1991).

GHITA EL KHAYAT
The Feminine Side of The Arab World (L'Harmattan, 1988).

FATIMA MERNISSI
The Prophet and Women (Albin Michel, 1987).
Cahiers Intersignes, n°1 : « Between Psychoanalysis and Islam »,
(Alef, 1990). *Cahiers d'Etudes Maghrébines,* n°1, 1990.

6

« IT IS NOT POWER THAT CORRUPTS, BUT FEAR »*

translated by Nina Mc Pherson

For the sixth time in its history, the Nobel Prize was awarded, on the 24th of October 1991, to a woman. And for the first time in its history — thanks to this same woman — it was awarded to a Burmese. A few months prior to the announcement of the award, on the 10th of July, Aung San Suu Kyi received the Sakharov Prize from the European Parliament. Unfortunately, she wasn't there to receive it. Aung San Suu Kyi is under house arrest, but even this expression delicately conceals the fact that she is being kept in absolute, solitary confinement somewhere in Burma, not far from the capital city of Rangoon.

It is with simplicity and deep emotion that Aung San Suu Kyi's husband, Michael Aris, introduces us, in the preface to an anthology of texts of which he is the editor, to a woman whose life takes the form of an odyssey from Rangoon to Rangoon, across India, England, Bhutan... like an epic, like a legend, an

---

* From *Freedom From Fear and Other Writings,* by AUNG SAN SUU KYI, Nobel Prize for Peace winner, 1991. (Penguin Books, and *Des femmes*, 1991)
A. Fouque wrote this article in *Passages* n°43, December 1991.

exemplary destiny, not only for the Burmese people, but for human history.*

Aung San Suu Kyi was born in 1945 in Rangoon, the Burmese capital, in a country which at the time was both ruled by the British and occupied by the Japanese. Her father, Aung San, the charismatic leader of the Burmese resistance, was assassinated in 1947, only shortly before his country gained its independence on January 4, 1948. In 1960, at the age of 15, Suu Kyi moves to New Delhi, India to live with her mother, the Burmese ambassador, a woman who also happens to be the first Burmese woman ever to become an ambassador for her country. Between 1964 and 1967, Suu Kyi studied political science at Saint Hugh's College, Oxford, where she ultimately earned her degree. In 1972, after working for several years for The United Nations Advisory Committee on Administrative and Budgetary Questions in New York, Suu Kyi married Michael Aris, a British Tibetologist from Oxford University and a specialist on Buddhist religion. Aung Sang Suu Kyi and Michael Aris have two sons.

From 1972 to 1988, Suu Kyi continued her graduate studies and travelled with her family from Bhutan to Japan to India, though always keeping London and Oxford as her moorings.

By 1984, Suu Kyi had finished and published a biography of her father entitled *Aung San of Burma*. In compiling in this book, the portrait of a man she never really knew, Suu Kyi sensed the inevitable, that she was to be his successor, « an icon of popular hope and longing » for the Burmese people. Or in the words of her husband, Michael Aris : « In the daughter as in the father there seems an extraordinary coin-

_____

* *Op.cit*

cidence of legend and reality, or word and deed. »*

In 1988, Suu Kyi was admitted to the School of Oriental and African Studies to pursue a doctorate in Burmese literature. At the time, she also dreamt of, and had begun to plan, the creation of an international study fellowship for Burmese students as well as a network of public libraries in Burma. But that same year, 1988, after receiving news that her mother Dan Khin Kyi, aged 70, was seriously ill, Suu Kyi returned home after 28 years in exile. Suu Kyi cared for her mother, the widow of a national hero, until her death in December 1988. On January 2, 1989, her mother's funeral attracted huge crowds; it was the only time, to date, that the Burmese government has ever cooperated with Suu Kyi.

Upon her return to Burma, Aung San Suu Kyi found not only an ailing mother, but an ailing country. Once the rice bowl of Asia, now a socialist republic in the throes of popular insurrection, Burma is a country which in economic terms has been bled white, ruined and starved by the incompetence and corruption of a « revolutionary » military junta, and torn apart by the ideological battles of its ethnic minorities and their struggle for recognition.

The French barely know Burma : this country of 40 million inhabitants, with a land area 25 percent larger than France, is bordered to the east by India and Bangladesh and to the west by China and Thailand, with the Himalayas to the north and the tropical sea of Adamal in the south. Enslaved by both the communist arms trade and the capitalist drug trade, Burma, which is one of the world's poorest countries, is also

---

* Introduction by Michael Aris, *op.cit.*

ruled by one of the world's most oppressive regimes. Burma is a country which has been closed off to journalists and humanitarian organizations for more than 30 years, a country which is run by means of torture, political intimidation, misery and fear. The Association France-Burma recently warned that prostitution — and, in the absence of condoms, all the associated risks — is spreading rapidly. The devastation of Burma's tropical forests continues to occur side by side with the cultivation of opium fields (the source of 90% of the heroin consumption in the United States). These two occupations help the Burmese regime finance its purchases of China's most sophisticated weaponry. On August 8, 1988, the Burmese government, an extreme nationalist socialist regime, a drug-trafficking dictatorship, puts down a popular insurrection in a blood bath.

This is the state of affairs, the backdrop to Aung San Suu Kyi's intuition, an intuition which will lead her to request a promise or a « favor » of her husband Michael Aris, before their marriage : « I only ask one thing, that should my people need me, you would help me to do my duty by them. »

This woman, who has remained so faithful to her primary identity, to the values and language of her country to the point of refusing to relinquish her Burmese citizenship and passport, and despite her marriage to an Englishman, only aspired to be worthy of her father's painful legacy : « As my father's daughter, I could not remain indifferent to the events in my country ; in effect, this national crisis can be considered the second independence struggle. »[*]

---

[*] *Ibid.*

For months, Burmese dissidents flocked to the house where Suu Kyi was then caring for her dying mother. Finally, on the 26th of August 1988, at the Shwedagon pagoda, a site of great symbolic importance in Burmese Buddhism, Suu Kyi spoke for the first time in public in front of a a crowd of hundreds of thousands of people. In the months that followed, Suu Kyi crisscrossed Burma — a country which was then and still is under martial law — insisting that the non-violent struggle for human rights and democracy be the first principal of the National League for Democracy, the party which she co-founded and now leads. As her husband described it : "She spoke to the Burmese as they had not been spoken to in so long, that is to say, as individuals worthy of love and respect. »*

On July 20, 1989, along with the majority of her fellow League members, Suu Kyi was placed under house arrest. However, despite a xenophobic government campaign against Suu Kyi (on the grounds that she was married to a British citizen and could thus never be a true national leader), her party won a landslide victory, carrying more than 80 percent of the votes. Again, her husband Michael Aris described the emotion and the irony of that moment: « The vote was a personal one for her : often the voters knew nothing about their candidate except that he represented Suu... There is a great irony in this, for she had become the focus of a personality cult which she would have been the first to decry. Loyalty to principles, she had often said, was more important than loyalty to individuals. »*

The military junta has never acknowledged that

* *Ibid.*

85

Aung San Suu Kyi won 80 percent of the votes.

Everything in Suu Kyi's life, the life of this serene woman, this woman who at a time of « frenetic activity » still made her house « a haven of love and care », this woman who for so many years had taken responsibility for her family so her husband could conduct his research, this woman who supported her husband and encouraged him in his work, everything would predispose Aung Sang Suu Kyi to sacrifice her peaceful family life, in the midst of great suffering, to be faithful to her mythic heritage, to become this « indomitable » heroine, this sage, this Mother Courage to a tyrannized people. This was the legacy of her parents, and it was both a paternal and a maternal legacy, masculine but feminine too, a legacy which drew on a deeply rooted Asian tradition of female leadership, from Indira Ghandi to Benazir Bhutto, on both Buddhist religious and cultural values and on Western democratic cultures founded on the spirit of the United Nations and the principles of human rights and — finally and perhaps most deeply — on the thought of Mahatma Gandi.

In her speech, *Freedom From Fear,* Aung San Suu Kyi's analysis of the origins of fear exposes unequivocally, the universal nature of fear, in Burma or elsewhere, even here, in France, where we are. « It is not power which corrupts but fear. The fear of losing power corrupts those who wield it and fear of the scourge of power corrupts those who are subject to it. »*

Vaclav Havel, who nominated Aung San Suu Kyi for the Nobel Prize, has also analyzed the phenomenon of fear under a communist regime: « Fear not in the

---

* *Op. cit.*

common, psychic sense, known as a concrete emotion » but « a profound fear... one which has an ethical
significance. »[1] The more brutal forms of oppression
— fear of trials, fear of torture, loss of property and
even deportation — have been replaced by more refined forms. The principal weight of this pressure has
now been displaced to the sphere of existence
where it becomes, in a certain sense, more universal : « Everyone loses something ; everyone has something to fear. »[1]

The greatest fear for the year 2000, as it was for the
year 1000, as it is today, is the fear of thought and
science, of the foreigner, of the Other, the green fear[2],
the brown fear, the fear of women, the misogynist
fear, the fear that undermines the fundamental liber-
ties and the sacred, inalienable rights of every human
being, regardless of their ethnic origin, their religion,
their nationality, their beliefs or their gender. Here, in
the West, from Austria to Louisiana, through Wallonie
and Scandinavia, this fear has given rise to young
chieftains who model themselves in the image of the
right-wing French politician Jean-Marie Le Pen.

If fear, East and West, can today be considered a universal simply because it is human, then a faithfulness
to oneself, a respect for one's fellow human beings,
the unrelenting effort, the resistance, the humble
daily gestures, the acute sense of responsibility, digni-
ty, and wisdom all shown by Aung San Suu Kyi, this
« indomitable » woman, may also become, through
her exemplary struggle, universal virtues, simply
because they too are human.

The daily asceticism, the daily ordeals, the courage
and wisdom which triumph over this fear and this
destructive madness — these are the non-violent gifts

which Aung San Suu Kyi has given us and the world, and which we must know to accept in order to wrest her from the shadows and the silence of her prison, so that we can give her back to those who love her and need her. If we are like children afraid of the dark, then in these shadowy times, the words of Suu Kyi light the way for us.

A political prisoner since June 1989, Aung San Suu Kyi has not been allowed to see her husband since December that same year, and the last letter her family received from her was dated July 17 1990. Today, international concern for her plight is immense. Last October, three members of the *Médecins du Monde* (Doctors Of The World) told the press that : « In reality, no one knows where she is being held. » (*Le Monde*, 19 octobre 1991).

NOTES

1. *Essais politiques* (Calmann-Levy), and *L'amour et la vérité doivent triompher de la haine et du mensonge* (Ed.de L'Aube), by Vaclav Havel.
2. *Contre La Peur*, by Dominique Lecourt (Ed. Hachette).

7

MY FREUD, MY FATHER *

translated by Nina Mc Pherson

If I try to conjure up the image of him I suffer from
diplopia : I see double. So I focus my vision and two
photos appear superimposed over the same image :
he is a small man, refined of appearance, even elegant ; outdoors, he always wore a hat. He is a man of
another generation. His gaze is piercing, painful ; it is,
at once, the gaze of a man and the gaze of a dog. I
create this tension by superimposing two portraits by
the same painter : the man-fruit and the man-book by
Archimboldo. One is the handsome Alexis, Virgil's faithful shepherd. But my father, he is the knight of the
Alliance, the adventurer ; they are more likely to have
been Abraham and Montaigne than Moses and Pascal.
These two men would have nothing in common, if

* Appeared in *Passages* n°46, April 1992, in the special dossier :
« Portrait of a civilized man : Freud ».

not for me, through whom their two names crossed in time, for the space of a story, in a book (Roudinesco[1]). Nevertheless, the worker and the thinker are both men of exile, of experience, of independence, men of honor, men of ethics more than of morals. At the heart of my memory and my unconscious, these two men will continue to play, work, think, and travel within me.

I remember now : I am three years old, it's a suffocating day in August ; my father takes me by the hand ; I trust him ; he takes me to a bull fight, the corrida. It is a real massacre ; I pee in my pants. From then on, I understand that all games are sexual and bloody, that joy for one person can mean suffering for another.

I am seventeen years old ; he is teaching me to drive, in his car, the one with the front-wheel drive.

I am thirty years old, and as familiar as this man is, the one who will lead me to the sphere of psychoanalysis, I side with the wild beast, our prehistory, wisdom through tears. Never will I be able to identify with the son who kills, in a gaudy suit, with the spectator who applauds, and who, generation after generation, has still never reached « The Age of Man ». He will try to offer me all his toys, all his concepts, or he will lend them to me and then take them back ; they will never be mine. He will want us to be contemporaries, so that fathers and daughters will become brothers and sisters — the eternal seduction.

« My little one, you have to see everything, do everything in life ». I was three years old ; I was thirty years old. He always offered it, the same invitation : « The important thing is to say everything ». I will learn the lesson, though without really making it my own. For me, the truth is divided. He knows, I believe, by communicating his passion to me, that my passion is not him. I am not at a loss for words or audacity, but I am not him : I am not even his « Filse »[2], his Antigone, half victim, half accomplice — even if, after yielding to the « object transfer » by having married, I have kept his initials, A.F. If he has landscaped a huge field of the savage country of my unconscious, he only knows the image he has made of me, which is still so very little. He doesn't entirely understand me ; he still hasn't decoded my « Linear A », my intimate handwriting.

I am proud of him, and my gratitude is infinite ; without him, I wouldn't be alive, I wouldn't be here in this world. But sometimes I am ashamed of him, when he wanted my sister to be a slave to his son, when he wanted my mother's love for her son to be unambivalent, when he pretended to speak for us ; he, the eternal son who pretended to ignore that the Father doesn't even exist.

Even if here where I live, he is still present, and always will be, we are definitely not contemporaries. Me, I belong to the Age of Women.

NOTES

1. Essay by Elisabeth Roudinesco : *The hundred-year battle : the history of psychoanalysis in France.* (Vol I, II), *Le Seuil*, 1986.
2. Cf. Women in movements, p.37.

DOCUMENT

THE WOMEN'S ALLIANCE
FOR DEMOCRATIZATION

translated by NINA MC PHERSON

We created the Women's Alliance for Democratization at the beginning of 1989 — the year of the bicentennial of the French Revolution and the Declaration of Human Rights — in order to give our movement a second and decisive momentum.

We have behind us 21 years of liberation struggles and we have ahead of us 10 years of work for democratization, to translate the experiments we have made into definitive goals, to integrate our thoughts and our actions, and to approach the history of the 21st century and the third millennium as adults.

Our democracy is far from being a true democracy, since women are for the most part excluded and are still far from enjoying a citizenship founded on their specific identity.

To work for democratization is to work so that history will acknowledge the existence of two sexes, and that this heterosexuality, this heterogeneity is the condition of the richness and the fertility of humanity ; it is to work so that the state of law will recognize the dyssymmetry between a woman and a man with respect to procreation and the affirmations that arise from this rather than endorsing a program for an ideal equality which will always elude us. An acknowledgment of the differences women present without equality will produce psychic regression and political reaction; equality without an acknowledgment of our differences, a sterile assimilation, a psycho-sexual amputation.

More than ever, we women will have to make complex gestures to achieve this notion of equality, to construct specific, but heterogeneous identities, to adapt ourselves without denying ourselves, to integrate ourselves while reintegrating our primary, sexual, original identity, and to create from this a mixed identity.

To put an end to the « derived libido », the « derived right », and the « derived identity », we will have to work from now to see that the legislators of language, symbol and law take our most vital demands into account. We must :

1/ Inscribe into the Constitution that « all human beings, of all sexes, races, religions or beliefs, possess equal and inalienable rights »

2/ Elaborate a blueprint law based on Universal Declaration of Women's Rights.

3/ Create and ensure the creation of more private time for women in order that they be thus empowered to take on greater political responsibilities.

4/ Gain recognition for women's specific forms of productivity. We are responsible for 100 percent of human procreation, but this production is excluded from all social, economic, professional, cultural and political recognition. This work is one of the last forms of slavery. Not only is this contribution, the greatest contribution of human richness to humanity, unrecognized and unpaid, but our undertaking of it can often penalize our professional activity and our creative work, despite the fact that procreation is recognized by creators as their model.

5/ Continue to train ourselves, to inform ourselves, to transmit and transform ourselves; to create new fields of knowledge, new sciences to enrich and articulate the pure and social sciences, to create an epistemological field : « sciences of women » — ranging from « Gyneconomy » to an elaboration of a specific « Body of Law ».

There are two sexes. This is a reality that the history of human rights, if it wants to be worthy of its ideals, must now adopt as its fourth principle, above even its liberty, equality and fraternity.

The women's movement has been and remains one of civi-

lization's most unifying and federative movements. It continues to spread through the entire world. It is more of a
transnational movement than an international movement,
which raises specific problems in each country but for
which the principles remain general and universal. The political choice of women has attained a planetary scale. It is in
such a context that it must take on a modern concept of the
rights of women, of their status and of their claim to a new
identity. This concept would engender solutions to some of
the most formidable problems which now threaten to
undermine democracy.

This democratisation work would not only benefit
women.

March 8th 1990.

CONTENTS